SAFE
AND
Alive

HOW TO PROTECT YOURSELF, YOUR FAMILY, AND YOUR PROPERTY AGAINST VIOLENCE

BY
TERRY DOBSON
with JUDITH SHEPHERD-CHOW

Published by J. P. Tarcher, Inc.
Los Angeles
Distributed by Houghton Mifflin Company
Boston

Library of Congress Cataloging in Publication Data

Dobson, Terry.
  Safe & alive.

  Bibliography: p. 150
  1. Crime prevention.   I.   Shepherd-Chow, Judith.
II.   Title.   III.   Title: Safe and alive.
HV7431.D6   362.8'7   81-9045
ISBN 0-87477-189-7   AACR2

    J. P. Tarcher, Inc.
    9110 Sunset Blvd.
    Los Angeles, CA 90069

Library of Congress Catalog Card No.: 81–9045

Design by Mike Yazzolino

Manufactured in the United States of America
S 10 9 8 7 6 5 4 3 2 1

First Edition

Dedicated to the memory of
Tom McCready
and his days at the Bond Street Dojo

Contents

Preface

The purpose of this book is to keep you out of harm's way. Its goal is to help you avoid becoming a victim both of violent crime and of the fears engendered by rising crime rates.

Americans of all walks of life are increasingly concerned about their personal safety. Although crime statistics vary greatly from one place to another, there is general agreement that the rates of murder, rape, and aggravated assault have risen dramatically in the last few years. In addition, due partly to the extensive and explicit crime coverage in daily newspapers and on TV news, many sense that the character of crime has grown steadily worse.

These acts of violence create an environment of fear, potentially as destructive as any authoritarian dictator. But they also present an opportunity to behave sensibly and responsibly on our own behalf. We have a larger stake than ever before in providing for our personal safety and the security of our loved ones. Fortunately, there is much that we can do, and that's the subject of this book.

Safe and Alive offers practical advice. First we describe the many steps you can take to thwart would-be assailants or intruders. Then we explain ways to reduce the risk of violence should it be impossible to foresee or avoid a particular situation. We want you to be able to choose the best, most appropriate, most life-sustaining response.

Many of these ideas and strategies will be familiar; for example, locking your car doors when you drive, or staying out of your home if, upon return, you have even the least suspicion that there might be intruders inside. But we feel these tried-and-true commonsense tips belong in any comprehensive discussion and are worth recounting, on the off chance that even one of them might be a brand-new idea for you.

We also move beyond the familiar. The spreading crime epidemic, again proving the old adage that necessity is the mother of invention, has inspired the development of sophisticated devices and strategies to protect yourself, your family, and your home. We'll describe many of these and evaluate their respective merits.

Use this book as a tool, reading it as though it were a scenario with yourself as the central performer. Analyze the situations you meet in the course of your daily life and your current modes of protection and patterns of behavior. You can then determine how you can change conditions that could potentially open you to danger.

Throughout the book we also give you opportunities for rehearsal in those situations that call for quick and intelligent responses. For example, what can you do if a threatening person joins you in an elevator, if you live alone and are awakened by strange noises in your living room, or if your car breaks down late at night in a high-crime neighborhood? We present some clear guidelines to improve your security, and give the options that are available when there isn't any one correct response.

We ask you to keep in mind that every encounter with a potentially dangerous person is unique, with its own priorities and variables, and that what works in one situation won't in another. For this reason, most threatening situations call for clearheadedness, intuition, and good judgment, so we emphasize how to remain in control in what are clearly difficult circumstances. One of the secondary benefits of adopting "safe and alive" behavior is reducing your level of fear. Preparation and prevention have the salutary effects of raising your self-confidence as well as increasing your chances for security.

Because *Safe and Alive* is a primer full of specific suggestions, some portions will be of greater interest and relevance to your life than others. Let the table of contents be your guide. Nevertheless, we urge you to read the epilogue, which includes a story that is a fable for our times.

We should note that this book does not cover every aspect of crime. For example, it isn't a sociological analysis of the reasons behind the rising crime rates. Nor is it a study of the root causes of criminal behavior. These are important subjects, worthy of your attention and interest, but they are not within the scope of this book.

Ms. Shepherd-Chow and I have also chosen to omit long discussions about preventing crimes against property, unless your personal safety is also involved, because other books have been devoted to this subject (see the Recommended Reading section at the end of the book). We've made a similar decision about the specifics of physical self-defense; again, much has been written elsewhere on this subject.

Regarding physical self-defense, however, I should note that my training and main field of interest for the past twenty years have been in the nonviolent resolution of conflict. I have been a student and teacher of Aikido, the Japanese martial art.

Aikido was developed by Morihei Ueshiba, a Japanese warrior who died in 1969 at the age of eighty-six. Drawing on ancient martial systems, Ueshiba developed a form of conflict response based on benevolence, the aim of which was peace, not domination. Central to his teaching is the idea that accommodation, not competition, is both the kindest and the most effective means of resolving a physical attack. Much from this art is applicable in our daily determination to avoid trouble. Therefore, we will introduce many of these ideas, especially in Part II of the book, which is devoted to preparedness.

Finally, we want to point out that any book dealing with criminal violence must emphasize the darker side of human nature. We think that any balanced and street-wise view of daily American life must record the innumerable acts of love, kindness, and sheer goodwill that people—both friends and strangers—do for each other every day. If there are violent criminals, there are also generous, wonderful people who will gladly give you a helping hand. If you pass up the opportunity to meet them, you miss a great deal of the best that life has to offer.

We want you to come away from reading this book alert to *whatever* life brings you, as ready to adapt to good fortune as to cope with bad luck, as aware of friendship and support as of potential danger and attack. We want you to be able to recognize the difference between prudence and paranoia, to be sensibly cautious while living the fullest life you possibly can. We want you to become—in the broadest sense—both safe *and* alive.

Acknowledgments

The authors wish to thank the following people for their advice and consultation in the preparation of this book:

Becky Balsam, Child and Adolescent Sexual Abuse Center, San Francisco General Hospital

Marcia Blackstock and Alegra Dashielle, Community Education and Training, Bay Area Women Against Rape

Dr. Stephen Blum, School of Public Health, University of California, Berkeley

Cyrus Carter and Thomas Bleecker, Out-Patient Services, Reality House West

Sgt. James A. Dachauer, San Francisco Police Department

Gerald G. Doane, Corporate Security, Crown Zellerbach

William H. Hayes, Department of Youth Authority, State of California

Capt. Richard D. Klapp, San Francisco Police Academy

Andrea Rechtin, Victim Consultation, Alameda County District Attorney's Office

Jacqueline Stanley, Criminal Justice Coordinating Council, New York City

We would also like to express our appreciation for the input and support of Laurie Chickering, Dan Chow, Shoshona Churgin, Cam Coe, Joe DeFazio, Kirsten Grimstad, Leigh Haber, Kimberly Hallet, Don Kates, Margo King, Victoria Kobayashi, George Leonard, George Pegelow, Eli Reed, David Rotman, Brian Van der Horst, and Veronique Vienne.

This book could not have come about without the wisdom of Jeremy Tarcher, and would not have come together without the splendid editorial direction of Millie Loeb.

Special gratitude is owed to Mr. Donn F. Draeger for his brief, kind, and exemplary instruction many years ago.

Despite the assistance of the people mentioned above, sole responsibility for the content of this book rests with its authors.

Terry Dobson
Judith Shepherd-Chow

"The only defense against the world is a thorough knowledge of it."

—JOHN LOCKE

Part One

Prevention: Taking Precautions Before Incidents Occur

The most important step you can take to protect yourself, your family, and your property from harm or destruction is to accept the fact that you are not immune to criminal violence. It can happen to anyone—and "it" can be anything from simple robbery to rape or murder. Part of this awareness concerns your psychological preparedness in the event of attack, and part involves the actions that can be taken to prevent attacks from occurring in the first place. These preventive measures will not hermetically seal you off from criminal activity, but the more precautions you take, the greater your chances of avoiding trouble.

Thus, we begin with precautions, those steps a prudent person can take to minimize the risk of harm, the proverbial stitch in time that saves nine. Realistically, this is bound to exact a certain amount of inconvenience and require a little extra effort, whether it means taking the trouble to install a front-door viewer or getting out of a warm bed to make sure all the doors are locked.

It may also involve a cash investment, the amount depending on your specific desires and circumstances. You could conceivably spend a fortune on personal and home security; in unusual situations (if, for example, you're the president of the United States or a superstar) this may be sensible, but for most of you it isn't necessary. Therefore, we emphasize the basic tools and equipment needed in every home, along with descriptions of more expensive and sophisticated systems if your lifestyle warrants these.

By taking preventive measures, you make a positive public statement. The very fact that you take the trouble says you care enough about yourself to provide for your safety. It says you don't see yourself as a victim.

Throughout Part I we explore the many procedures, techniques, tips, and devices that can help you prevent crime from invading your life. They can be divided into the following categories, which are the subjects of the first four chapters:

1. *Precautions in Public*—ways to avoid attack on the streets and in public places.

2. *In the Privacy of Your Home*—at-home safety routines, the steps you should take almost automatically, both in normal circumstances and in emergency situations.

3. *Protecting Your Home and Car*—techniques and devices to prevent unauthorized entry or attack.

4. *Getting Special Instruction*—suggestions concerning anticrime instruction in your community.

Chapter One

Precautions in Public

1 Not Looking Like a Victim

In this chapter we will focus on the many ways you can protect yourself in public, whether visiting the local grocery store or on a tour of Europe. There are more than 150 suggestions in this chapter alone, so as you read you might want to mark the ones you find especially useful.

In public, the best way to avoid attack is to present yourself in a manner that discourages would-be assailants. It's as though we send out messages telling others that their attack is either likely or unlikely to be resisted.

Through body language and general attitude, the victim sends a subtle yet unmistakable message to the mugger. It says something like "Please don't attack me! I'm so afraid." To a mugger, the most impulsive of criminals, this communication is tantamount to an engraved invitation. Expecting no opposition, he moves in immediately.

The conclusion is inescapable: *You must show yourself as someone with self-worth, someone who cares what happens and will mount a vigorous defense if attacked.* This is not to suggest that you walk around looking tough or that you should challenge anyone on the street. But you must be alert in public situations, presenting yourself in such a way that predatory strangers see you as a high-risk target.

You can have a positive public image by following a few simple guidelines:

1. Walk briskly, with an air of self-confidence and purpose. Stand up to your full measure, keeping your center of gravity low and your head level. Fix your eyes on a distant horizon and imagine that you're being gently pulled toward it.

2. Look as if you know where you are heading even if you are a bit lost. If you must venture into an unfamiliar neighborhood, get detailed directions beforehand. If you are lost and need directions, seek help from a police officer, a store clerk, or a gas station attendant.

3. Stay awake on public transportation.

4. Learn by observing others on the street. You can do this most easily while sitting in a sidewalk cafe or by standing in a movie line. Notice the subtle differences we have described and practice the body stances of those who appear the strongest and least vulnerable.

5. On bad days, maintain a low profile. Face up to those times when it is difficult to project a positive image—alert, self-confident, with a lively step and erect posture. You may feel ill, depressed, or unhappy, or you may just be having a bad day. During such times try, if possible, to restrict your movements.

See Section 4, "Street-Smart Behavior," in this chapter for additional advice.

---

2 Restricting Personal Information

When we lived in small communities and neighborhoods where everyone knew one another, doors were left open and children and neighbors wandered freely in and out. Understandably, these carefree environments lent themselves to an open sharing of facts about ourselves.

We've learned to lock our doors, but—in a spirit of openness or forgetfulness—we are often indiscreet about providing information to strangers and acquaintances that could be of value should they wish to do us harm. Just because you have nothing to hide, it doesn't follow that everybody should know your personal business. A few simple precautions can prevent many problems.

Make it a habit to restrict the following kinds of information unless you specifically want others to know·

1. Who you are.

2. Where you live.

3. What you do for a living.

4. What your habits and routines are.

5. How much you're worth.

Who You Are

1. You are under no obligation to tell a stranger your name or, if pressed, your correct name. Chances are the request is a harmless one, but the point is that it should be up to you to decide whether you want to give out the information. You can also ask household help and co-workers to be similarly discreet.

2. Your public image counts. The way you look and present yourself is another basic way of saying who you are. Your general appearance tells people immediately how you see yourself. If you're neat and tidy, the general impression is that you care about yourself. If you're sloppy, you come across as somewhat indifferent about what happens to you—in other words, an easy target. Whether it's fair or not, you should recognize that people—even would-be assailants—judge you by your appearance. Their judgment may be totally wrong, but judge you they will.

3. Dress to avoid problems. The way you dress is extremely important in terms of attracting or discouraging attention. You have every right, of course, to dress any way you want. If you're a young man and wish to display the thousand-dollar

wristwatch your rich uncle gave you as a graduation present, you have every right to do so. If you're a woman who wants to wear tight, short shorts and a revealing halter top, that's your right too. The realities of modern American life, however, suggest that you choose the "right" time and place for these displays. On your own turf, so to speak, among your friends, you will probably attract welcome attention, but in unfamiliar neighborhoods or on public streets these displays are almost guaranteed to bring you the wrong kind of attention. Some men will presume that a woman's revealing attire is an invitation to harassment or worse—that she's "asking for it." Similarly, someone may presume that "any man dumb enough to wear a watch like that around here deserves to have it stolen." So, regardless of your right to wear whatever you please, if you want to discourage unwanted attention, conceal yourself, your jewelry, your watch, your camera, and any other valuables.

Where You Live

1. Be especially cautious about giving out your address or phone number indiscriminately. This is always wise, but especially so if you live alone (in Chapter Two we will discuss some strategies for disguising this fact and for foiling the telephone intruder).

2. If you suspect that someone is following you home, drive past and go immediately to a safe location, preferably to the nearest police or fire station or to a public place where people are congregated.

What You Do for a Living

1. Keep a low profile unless you're a politician running for office. You don't have to tell strangers what you do, any more than you have to tell them anything else. Most people who ask "What do you do for a living?" are just making conversation. But if you work for a jeweler or a bank or in any kind of sensitive position, there might be an ulterior motive to such questioning. How can you tell? You'll have to rely on your intuition to help you distinguish between genuine social interest and masked hustling. If the inquiring individuals seem more bent

on interrogating you than on sharing and exchanging information, be on the alert.

2. Carry business cards that do not include your home address or phone number. Use these cards if you wish additional contact either for business or personal reasons, but be selective in giving them out. Never leave a stack on a table or let someone else pass them out. If you're discarding old cards, rip them in pieces first.

3. Instruct co-workers not to divulge your home phone number or address unless they have explicit instructions to do so.

4. If you use your home as your place of business, the most security-minded approach is to rent a post office box. You can also list your phone number without an address in the phone book.

5. Hire a professional telephone-answering service, if you can afford it, or install a phone-answering machine.

Your Habits and Routines

In a street-wise view of things, predictability can equal vulnerability. If someone who wishes to harm you knows what you're going to do, the odds are that this person can plan for these contingencies. For example, if he knows you're in the Bahamas on vacation, your home becomes a more likely target.

Here are two important points to keep in mind.

1. Cultivate unpredictability in both your daily movements and special activities. Vary the way you do things—don't walk the same route to your bus stop in the morning; don't leave home for work or go to the bank at the same time every day. Varying your habits keeps you on your toes, aware of the ruts of personal behavior that groove the surface of your life. It also makes it more difficult for a potential burglar or assailant to get a fix on you and thus figure out where you'll be when.

2. Conversely, develop safety habits. Many habits are protective. Checking the back seat of your car at night before getting in is one example; making sure your house and windows or screens are locked before you go to bed is another. We'll discuss this in

more detail in subsequent chapters, but the important thing to keep in mind is to restrict knowledge of your behavior patterns to those people whom you trust.

How Much You're Worth

If you live in an upper-income neighborhood or are in certain professions, both acquaintances and strangers will assume that you are wealthy even if this isn't the case. Crying poverty is limited as a strategy since most would-be burglars are not likely to be in your social circle.

Nevertheless, there are some guidelines for restricting information that can be helpful to anyone with cash or possessions worth protecting.

1. Except to comply with the law, don't tell anyone but your closest friends and relatives how much money you or your spouse earns or what you have in the way of expensive possessions. Recent or planned purchases can be very exciting, but don't brag about them. This also holds true for your fabulous art or coin collection. If you have an expensive car—which means almost any new car today—it's best to keep it in a locked garage, not in your driveway.

2. Keep a low profile in public. This is where as many as 90 percent of muggings occur spontaneously. Women in big cities have learned not to wear gold chains and other expensive jewelry on the street since this makes them immediate targets. Now that it's become fashionable for men to wear jewelry, they must also learn to be cautious.

3. Be careful when making purchases. It's smart not to have too much money visible in your wallet or purse when you pay for something in a store. If you're carrying a lot of cash (which we don't advise), divide the bills and carry them in different places.

4. Be discreet with strangers. Don't tell them that the bank president is your father or that you carry every credit card imaginable. In short, keep money talk to a minimum.

3 Tools of Self-Protection

An almost limitless number of devices can be used for self-protection. Whatever their nature, they tend to fall into the following categories:

Weapons

For our purposes, we will use the word "weapon" to refer to any artifact or device made primarily for use in the incapacitation or control of one person by another. This category includes firearms (primarily handguns) and aerosol tear-gas propellants, which have no real function except for personal protection.

Correct use of a weapon requires three things: constant practice, maintenance, and a cool head. Without practice, you won't be able to handle your weapon; without maintenance, the weapon won't work; without a cool head, you won't hit your target. Unless you fully meet these three requirements, you are potentially a danger to both yourself and others.

Practically speaking, most weapons are mechanical delivery systems—that is, they deliver a payload across an intervening space at a (usually moving) target. The advantages of these systems are their reach, stopping power, and deterrent effect (if one can "get the drop on" an assailant). The disadvantages are the amount of training required to become proficient, the time it takes to retrieve the weapon from its place of concealment, the possibility of malfunction, the chance that a child will play with it or that someone will use it against you, and the legal strictures against possession and use.

We also have reservations about tear gas, which is marketed under a number of brand names, including Mace. The typical training period of two or three hours is not long enough to become thoroughly familiar with something that might save your life. With any tear-gas device, we recommend additional training (perhaps in the martial arts) to develop the mental control necessary to use the weapon effectively in situations of high stress and rapid movement.

We do not favor reliance on handguns for self-defense, except in rare and exceptional circumstances, which only you can determine. We feel the shooting of one human being by another is an ugly, brutal, degrading event for both persons. If a firearm is used against a person, it should be used only *in extremis,* after all other available protective measures have been exhausted. However, if you already own a gun or decide to purchase one, you should fully understand the firearms law in your community and state, and be fully informed about ethical considerations in using weapons for self-defense. For information about weapons instruction, see Chapter Four.

Everyday Objects

Many ordinary items can be used for self-defense in an emergency—a pencil or pen, a handful of coins, a bottle, a baseball bat, a door, a car, a bowl of soup, your keys. Be prepared to make use of whatever the particular environment offers as a protective aid.

Using everyday objects as self-protective tools requires little more than the pure intention to preserve life. Armed with this spirit, you will be able to seize nearly any nearby object to help you stay safe and alive.

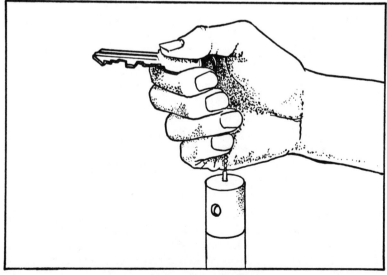

How to hold your keys (note shriek alarm attached).

Although anything can be used for protection, it's wise to think ahead. Examine the objects you normally carry, projecting situations in which each might be used defensively. The coins you carry in your pocket or purse, for example, could be flung at an attacker's face with great force; the can of oven cleaner or spray paint you just bought at the supermarket could blind an assailant long enough for you to get away. The list is endless, but the most important point is your desire to live and your willingness to use no more force than absolutely necessary to prevent injury to yourself; using excessive force means that *you* have become the attacker.

Noisemakers

This category includes police whistles, shriek alarms, bull horns—anything that can be used to make noise or summon help. (See Section 4, "Street-Smart Behavior," for a discussion of your voice as a tool of self-protection.) One of the major advantages of these devices is that they can't be used against you.

Keep an extra shriek alarm or police whistle in your car, because the need to make noise or summon assistance is not limited to situations where you are the victim; you can use it to call for help if you see someone else being attacked.

Using Protective Devices

More important than any technical distinction among these categories is your attitude, intention, and spirit when you use a tool. If your attitude is flighty, your intent wavering, or your spirit weak, you will not be able to use any device with telling effect. Every year we hear about seasoned police officers shooting at felons at close range without hitting them, presumably because of excitement or fear.

Therefore, there are three primary points to keep in mind when using self-protective tools.

1. Maximize the effectiveness of whatever tool you select. Some serve to channel a comparatively large amount of force through small points of impact. Others deflect or hinder movement. Whatever the object, it has its own utility—concentrate all your energy on using it correctly in the situation.

2. Move against your assailant's weakness. Rather than trying to counter your assailant's strengths, employ the tool against his weakest points. Don't be squeamish, as causing your attacker some pain may be the quickest and most humane way of minimizing injury and restoring peace. The "minimum force" required of you in a particular situation might normally be considered very violent behavior. If it is necessary to save your life, do it without reservation.

3. Once you've decided to employ a particular tool, use it with total vigor and commitment. Don't hesitate and don't quit unless and until your assailant is immobile, has given up all resistance, or has run away. Anything less than an all-out effort will probably be unsuccessful—and success can be judged only when the danger has passed.

How to Face a Weapon

Facing a criminal with a weapon demands courage and self-possession. It is an extremely dangerous and frightening encounter. We can offer no easy answers, but we can help you be prepared. Forethought and readiness can avert panic. It is essential to remain coolheaded in this type of emergency. Memorize the following basic guidelines:

1. When the person threatening you has a visible weapon, take all threats literally. If an assailant has a gun and says, "Don't move or I'll shoot!" take the statement as gospel. At the same time, consider it a statement of dual intent—that is: if you move, I will shoot; if you don't move, I won't. If, however, your attacker starts shooting anyway (either at you or at someone else) —*move!* Duck for cover or escape.

2. If you hear gunshots, drop to the ground or floor. Then find cover under or behind something as soon as possible.

3. If you face a person with a weapon, look at the person, not at the weapon. By itself, the weapon can't do anything; your problem is not with the weapon but with the person who holds it. Therefore, make and maintain eye contact. Speak quietly and reassuringly. Try to calm and soothe him by providing assurance that he has nothing to fear from you. This is especially important with someone under the influence of drugs or

alcohol or someone having a "psychotic episode" or a break with reality. Such people may be easily excited and see danger multiplying around them. Although a gun is inanimate, it has a tremendous power of attraction because of its death-dealing potential. Resist all temptation to look head-on at the muzzle of a pointed gun. It is like looking down a deep, dark tunnel, and it can terrify and immobilize you.

4. If an armed assailant wants to force you to accompany him from a comparatively public place to a comparatively secluded place, it may—repeat, may—be the wisest course of action to refuse to go. If you refuse, you run the risk of his using the weapon and injuring you. Nonetheless, if your attacker uses his weapon in public, where your rescue and his apprehension is likely, it's a cinch he'd have used it where no one could see him and where he could take his time. You will, obviously, have to judge the situation on its own merits, but the general rule about captivity is that the longer you're held, the harder it is to escape.

5. Your short-term objective is to control the weapon or put yourself out of its range. There are two ways to accomplish this. One is physically to move your body around behind the weapon; the other is to persuade the gunman to turn it away from you. Your chances of accomplishing the latter are much greater, especially if you are calm and collected.

---

4 Street-Smart Behavior

As we have already noted, there are a number of things you can do about your personal image to reduce the chances of being harmed while walking on city streets. We focus here on other ways to protect yourself in these circumstances.

1. Whenever possible, walk with a friend. Surveys indicate that you can reduce your chances of being attacked by nearly 70 percent if you walk with another person, and by 90 percent if

you're with two others. If you're elderly or handicapped, or just generally not up to par, arrange to go shopping and do errands with friends. Some communities provide an escort service for senior citizens. Check with your local church or senior citizens' center to see if there is such a service in your neighborhood.

2. Walk purposefully. Unless you're in a neighborhood you know well, walk, don't stroll. Look as if you've got somewhere to go and are very determined to get there soon—head up, eyes focused, step snappy. This is particularly important in a neighborhood with numbers of people loitering on the street. Don't pretend you're invisible. Look as if you have something to accomplish and will be on your way directly. You may not escape notice, but you should look like you mean business.

3. Limit your contact with strangers on the street. Even if one or more persons block your path, look right through them with a neutral gaze, as if they didn't exist. Your errand is infinitely more important than anything they have to tell you, and your expression should communicate that message. This doesn't mean you should look at them with contempt or superciliousness, which will cause them to respond with hostility, but only as though you have no time and no change to spare.

4. At night, walk in open places or places that are well-lighted. This is no ironclad assurance of safety, but your chances are much more favorable. If you have to be where there are no other people around at night, walk in the middle of the street so that a mugger or rapist can't easily jump you from behind a parked car or bushes. Stay clear of any place where someone could be concealed and take you by surprise.

5. Carry a good flashlight in your purse or in your car. This will be helpful if you're ever stranded on a darkened street at night, as a flashlight can help you detect potential assailants and can also function as a defense tool if necessary.

6. Avoid shortcuts through parks, tunnels, parking lots, and alleys. In fact, it's best to stick to main thoroughfares whenever possible. It might take you a bit longer to get to your destination, but it's worth the effort.

7. Be alert on the street. Observe what's going on around you. This is especially good advice if you are in an unfamiliar neighborhood, if you tend to walk around lost in thought, or if you become absorbed in conversation with a friend. In a major shopping center in Los Angeles, business tenants have been advised to be wary of people who are acting oddly or are dressed outrageously, because they often serve as diversions from the commission of a crime. If you should find yourself attracted to something happening on the street, that's the time to hold your purse a bit more tightly and move away from whatever is going on.

8. Carry two or three spare dimes. If this money is readily available, you can usually reach help in an emergency if you can get to a phone booth. In fact, a closed phone booth can be a temporary island of safety if you sit on the floor with your feet against the door.

9. Check with your local police to see if there is a 911 emergency number. In many large cities (for example, New York, Chicago, Philadelphia, Boston, Washington, D.C., Detroit, Miami, Denver, and Seattle)—and in others to come—911 is set aside for this purpose and can be called without a dime.

10. Don't carry a purse. The Syracuse Police Department has advised local women to wear clothes with pockets to eliminate the need for carrying a purse. This tactic has dramatically reduced the number of purse snatchings in that city and should be especially helpful for senior citizens.

11. If you must carry a purse, briefcase, or packages, hold them tightly and close to your body. Carry a purse that closes with a zipper or snaps, because it is a less appealing target. Keep the flap or opening next to your body. Also, wrapping the strap of the purse around your wrist several times makes you look like someone who has considered the possibility of purse snatching and is prepared to resist. A would-be assailant may well look for an easier victim.

12. Don't carry more cash or credit cards than you actually need. Before you leave home, spend a few moments planning your errands, and take only those gas and credit cards you'll need or that would be useful in an emergency. Keep a list (at home or in

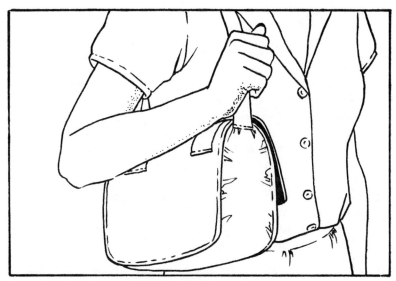

Keep flap side of your purse close to your body.

your office) of all your credit cards and their account numbers, as well as the phone numbers to call if they are lost or stolen. Most experts advise you to carry a small amount of cash—five or ten dollars—since some muggers become violent if they are forced to go away empty-handed.

13. Be extra alert in boundary zones. For our purposes, a boundary zone is the area you must traverse between any two places—between, say, your house and your car, the elevator of your office building and the street, your neighborhood and the one next to it. Many crimes occur in these zones, so be especially alert when you are in them. Always have your keys in your hand when you approach your house or car, and be alert for strangers. At the same time, don't be in such a hurry that you fail to check whether it's safe to enter. Make sure that the door hasn't already been forced, and that there's no one hiding under or in your car. If possible, walk to your car or to public transportation with another person when you leave work.

14. When moving from an area of light into darkness, stop for a few moments and let your eyes adjust. This applies when entering movie theaters, for example; try to stand in the back for a moment to let your eyes adjust so that you can pick the seats

you want. When leaving, let your eyes adjust to the lighted lobby before going outdoors.

15. Carry a shriek alarm or a police whistle. If somebody bothers you on the street, the noise you make will both attract attention and frighten your attacker. A shriek alarm is preferable to a whistle, because it creates a piercing sound and does not require you to take deep breaths. Attach either of these objects to your key ring to have it at hand when needed, not absentmindedly left behind or lost at the bottom of your purse. You might not need a shriek alarm in your hand on a busy street in broad daylight, but ready it when you move to less-traveled streets or are about to enter your house or apartment building, especially at night. It is important to understand the shock value of a loud sound at close range. A sudden burst of official-sounding shrieks will turn just about anybody around in their tracks.

16. Keep in mind that your voice is a tool of self-protection. If attacked, let out the most piercing, most glass-shattering scream you can muster, aiming it right between your attacker's eyes. Don't stop until he has fled or help has arrived. If your assailant flees, change your scream from sheer sound to specific words: "Help! Police! Murder!" or "Stop, thief!" This alerts people to the specific nature of the crime and may prompt reports to the police. Even if you think your cries may not be heard, scream anyway—and speak loudly to your assailant. The volume communicates personal strength and the seriousness of your intention. Avoid questions such as "What do you think you're doing?" or "Who do you think you are?" They are weaker than direct orders: "Stop!" or "Get out of here!" or "Leave me alone!" In this way you reinforce your authority.

17. If someone grabs your purse or other property, and conditions are such that it's not wise to fight (see Chapter Six), let go of the article and drop to one knee. This position protects you in case your attacker tries to knock you down, and it also makes it easier to ward off blows and kicks. Keep in mind that your primary goal is not to protect your money and property. These are replaceable. If conversation with your assailant is possible, tell him you hope what he's taken is of help to him. This graciousness can reduce your risk of harm.

5 Security in Your Car or on Public Transportation

Below are commonsense safety strategies to follow then driving your car. Later in the chapter we'll take up safety in the use of public transportation.

In Your Car

1. Keep your car well equipped and in good running order. Have your car serviced regularly, following the suggestions in your owner's manual. (If you don't have this booklet, obtain one from your local dealer or ask him for advice.) Check your tires' air pressure on a regular basis—at least twice a month. Carry a quart of motor oil and keep your gas tank at least a quarter full to reduce the possibility of being stranded. Carry the following equipment in your car's trunk: a jack, a basic tool kit, flares, a blanket, matches, an umbrella, and a spare tire that's in good condition. Keep a flashlight and appropriate maps in your glove compartment.

2. Lock your car doors, both when you leave it and when you drive. The dramatic rise in car thefts has been accompanied by an increase in "traffic light" robberies: someone runs up to a car stopped for a light, yanks open an unlocked door, pummels the driver, and takes his or her money. To forestall this, keep the doors locked and the windows rolled up far enough so that no one can slip in an arm to unlock the door. If you have a hatchback vehicle, keep this window locked as well.

3. Stick to main thoroughfares after dark. Don't take shortcuts on dark, untraveled routes. Not only would it be hard to summon help if you had car trouble, but you would also be a sitting duck.

4. Park as close to your destination as possible, especially at night. Avoid remote or underground parking lots where possible. If you can't do so and must return to your car alone, either take off your shoes and move quickly and silently to your car, or talk loudly and gaily to the (imaginary) friends who are

following you at a distance. The best practice is to wait at the entrance to the lot until the parking attendant or some other trustworthy person can escort you.

5. When you park at night, look for a well-lighted location. Before you park your car, check to see if there are any suspicious people about, either on the street or sitting in parked cars. If there are, find another place to park. In general, it's better to park your car in an outdoor parking lot than on a street. If you park in a public lot, don't tell the attendant how long you will be gone. If you must leave your key, leave only your ignition key, not your trunk key, and by all means not your house key. Any drugstore, hardware store, or locksmith carries the sort of key ring that lets you easily detach your ignition key from the others.

6. Keep your doors locked and stay with your car if you have car trouble. Pull over to the right, as far off the road as possible, and stop. Hang a white handkerchief or rag on your radio antenna as a distress signal. Don't go for help unless there are extenuating circumstances of a critical nature—for example, you've run out of gas in below-zero weather, are in danger of freezing to death, and see a farmhouse nearby. If you must, leave a note stating the trouble, where you've gone, when you left, and who you are. This will notify police that the car has not been abandoned.

7. Do not stay with your vehicle if you develop car trouble on a freeway and are unable to move the car to the shoulder. Try to place lights or flares far enough behind your car to alert other motorists to the stalled car ahead. If it's too dangerous to stand in the road looking for a flare or flashlight in the trunk, get on the right side of the road and walk back toward the traffic, waving a coat or shirt to flag down oncoming cars.

8. If someone stops to offer assistance, ask them to call the highway patrol, the local police, or the auto club. If you're a member, give them your number. Unless your life is endangered by staying with your car, don't get in anyone else's car. Speak from inside your locked car, with the window rolled down just enough to communicate.

9. If you get a flat tire in a hazardous part of the road or a dangerous part of town, don't stop to fix it there. Keep on driving slowly until you find a place that's safe to stop. It may cost you a tire or even a wheel rim, but it's better than risking your life.

10. Don't stop to render direct assistance to another motorist if you're alone. Even if you're not alone, use extreme caution. Pull over fifty to a hundred yards past the stopped car, and then back up slowly until you can shout to its occupant to ascertain the trouble. Keep your doors locked and roll down the windows only enough to be heard. If anyone moves toward you in a way that arouses your suspicion, step on the gas and leave immediately. Try to remember the license-plate number of the other car, and report the incident to the police immediately. Even if you come upon what looks like an accident, don't let down your guard. Faking accidents in order to rob and assault people who stop to help is an ancient tactic. If you do see someone in trouble on the road, however, the decent thing to do is to stop at the nearest telephone and inform the highway patrol or local police. (See Section 41, "Becoming a 'Safe and Alive' Good Samaritan," in Chapter Eight.)

11. Don't pick up hitchhikers. Too many people have been victimized by trying to help innocent-looking people pretending to need a lift.

12. Don't argue with other drivers. Each of you is driving what can be a lethal weapon. If another driver cuts you off or is otherwise rude or insulting, don't take it upon yourself to teach him the error of his ways. Somebody else will do that. Let him go ahead of you. Many people work out their anger as they drive; sometimes they won't dim their headlights at night, or they lower them and then switch to high beam when they're right in front of you. Don't let them get your goat.

Public Transportation

Whether it be subway, taxi, train, bus, or jumbo jet, public transportation poses some unique perils. As a first precaution, check for possible schedule changes to limit the amount of time you must wait, especially at night.

Guidelines for Waiting

1. When waiting in a deserted place, have a shriek alarm or police whistle handy.

2. Be alert while waiting. Don't get so deeply involved in reading a magazine or newspaper that you fail to notice a person approaching.

3. Stand in the shadows if it's dark and you're the only person waiting. Ideally, stand where you can see the bus when it comes but cannot be easily seen by passersby in cars.

4. Move away from trouble calmly and quickly. For example, you don't have to stay on the platform of a subway station or at a bus stop if a menacing drunk is present.

5. When waiting for a subway train, stand near the most-used entrance or the ticket booth. Never stand right at the edge of the platform. Plan to ride in the trainman's car (usually in the middle of the train) and, if possible, gauge where this car will stop so that you can board quickly.

6. Don't get off at your destination if it's deserted and your intuition tells you that another passenger may attempt to follow you. Simply continue to the nearest stop where you can get off safely and call a cab or where you can get another train or bus to take you back to your original destination.

7. When waiting for an airplane, be alert for two possible sources of trouble—terrorist activity and pickpocketing. Stay away from baggage lockers, since they have been known to contain explosive devices. In the airport of a country experiencing social or political unrest, try to avoid waiting in its lounge. If you cannot, be ready to take shelter in the event of a sudden disturbance. Also be alert for pickpockets, who know that you may be carrying substantial sums of vacation money or jewelry. They watch for travelers whose minds may be miles away—at the place they're heading for or from which they've just returned. (See Section 8, "Travel Guidelines," in this chapter.)

8. Don't accept rides from strangers. Waiting for a bus or other transportation from an airport into the city can be tedious.

Nevertheless, resist the temptation to save time or money by sharing a cab with strangers or accepting a free ride. The prudent person will wait for the limousine, the bus, or the taxi, no matter how long it takes.

Guidelines for Riding

1. Don't sit right next to the door. Frequently, thieves will dash in, grab a purse, and then disappear just as the doors close. On buses, subways, and trains, always sit in an aisle seat so that you can get up easily and summon help if someone bothers you.

2. It's unwise to sleep on public transportation, particularly local vehicles. On longer trips, where it may be difficult to stay awake, make sure your portable luggage is stowed close to you so that anyone tampering with it will awaken you immediately.

3. Be especially alert when traveling during rush hours or holiday seasons. Tempers are more likely to flare at these times, and pockets are more apt to be picked. If you can arrange your schedule to travel at other times, by all means do so.

4. Hold on firmly to your purse or briefcase. Don't put it on the seat beside you. Hold it in your lap or wedge it between your feet.

5. Keep your young children in sight at all times. On an airplane, accompany them to the restroom.

6. When using taxis, special guidelines should be followed. Most drivers are honest, but precautionary behavior can protect you from the exceptions.

    a. Never get into an unlicensed "gypsy" cab. Licensed cabs are required to post the driver's identification, with photo, where it is visible to passengers. Make sure the identification matches the driver of the cab.

    b. Make a note of the driver's name at the beginning of the trip.

    c. Don't reveal any unnecessary personal information to cab drivers. For example, don't tell them what you do or anything that might lead them to see your home as a possibility for burglary. If a cab picks you up at home to take you to the airport or bus or train station, imply that your trip will be brief and that your home will be occupied during your absence.

d. If a taxi driver makes sexual advances, don't alert him to your intent but get out of the cab at the first stop sign or stop light and notify the police—even if you must leave your luggage behind.

---

6 Playing It Safe

It's easy to let your guard down when you go out to have a good time. Criminals know this, so these are the very times when some extra safety measures are imperative. We have organized them according to the places you might visit.

Beaches and Parks

1. Plan outings with at least one other friend. In fact, the more the merrier—and the safer. With one or more companions, each person can take a turn watching the valuables while others swim, doze off, run, or get refreshments. We recommend using the buddy system when swimming. It's also helpful if someone in your party is familiar with the area you're visiting.

2. In parks, stay on well-traveled paths. At beaches and parks, stay where other people are congregated.

3. Leave extra money and credit cards at home. Be similarly cautious with your other valuables.

4. Move to another area if you're near a group of people who are becoming boisterous or out of line.

5. At the beach, settle near a lifeguard station.

6. If you have a dog, take it with you on a leash unless local ordinances don't permit you to do so.

7. Stay away from places where there has been recent trouble. Keep informed, through the news media, about what's happening in various parts of your community. If you have any doubts about the safety of a particular area, check with the police.

8. Take along your shriek alarm or police whistle and follow the same precautions you would on the street.

9. Stay away from parks and beaches at night. No matter how pleasant these places are, it's not worth the risk unless you're going to an organized party with many others invited. Even in these circumstances, be especially cautious going to and from your car or public transportation.

Arenas and Theaters

1. Keep your valuables on your lap for safekeeping. Don't put a purse or packages in the next seat—an adept thief behind you can manipulate the empty seat so that your bag or package slips through the space between the seat and the backrest.

2. Be alert when entering public restrooms. Don't go in if you see someone suspicious. It's also a good idea to have a shriek alarm handy, especially if you must use the restroom during a performance.

3. Check the theater's or arena's emergency exits when you come in. Make sure you know what route to take in the event of a disturbance or emergency.

4. If trouble breaks out, leave quickly, and make sure the rest of your party leaves too.

5. If you become caught in a press of people, don't struggle. Relax and try to flow with the movement (see Section 26 in Chapter Five—"Gaining and Regaining Your Composure"). When you can do so easily, move toward the outside wall of the room or enclosure.

Hiking and Jogging

Hiking or jogging, especially in natural settings, can be good for both body and soul. At the same time, however, you must remain alert to danger.

1. Hike or jog with a partner.
2. Choose a well-traveled trail.
3. Don't hike or jog after dark.
4. Don't hike or jog the same trails at the same time of day, day of week, etc. Vary your routine to discourage surveillance.
5. If you can, walk or run with a dog. If you can't, carry a shriek alarm.

---

7 Safety in Stores or Office Buildings

In Stores

Shopping or doing errands calls for special precautions to reduce your chances of being involved in either an unpleasant or a violent confrontation. Each of these measures can make a difference:

1. Always keep your purse with you. If you leave it in your grocery cart when you wander away to squeeze the Charmin or inspect the fruit, you're inviting trouble. Similarly, don't leave it in a department store dressing room when you go to look for more merchandise. Thieves who pose as patrons will exploit this error.

2. Handle money in public with caution and discretion. Professional thieves are attracted to people with a large amount of bills. Follow the travel guidelines suggested in Section 8 of this chapter.

3. As you enter a store or bank, quickly observe what's going on. If anything seems unusual or suspicious, leave immediately and notify the authorities.

4. Be especially vigilant during the holiday season, since this is a time when criminal activity increases.

5. Don't carry too many bundles. If your arms are full, you will inevitably become more vulnerable. Most stores are willing to mail or deliver packages to your home or office. Take advantage of this service.

6. Carry purchases in your own shopping tote, not one bearing the logo of a luxury-priced store. You become a more attractive target on the street or on public transportation if a would-be assailant believes you're carrying something of value.

7. Avoid using on-the-sidewalk mechanical bank tellers, especially after dark, unless you absolutely must. If you're using one of these machines, punch in the wrong code if someone even vaguely suspicious is lurking nearby. Then pretend you can't remember the right combination of numbers.

8. Patronize self-service establishments such as laundromats or gas stations only during daylight hours.

In Office Buildings

1. If you are a visitor, follow the same precautions you would when entering any store or bank. (See number 5 below on elevator safety.)

2. Don't use the stairways unless there is a fire or some other emergency. You may have to wait a few minutes for an elevator, but patience is your best protection.

3. Keep your purse under lock and key. Office robberies are very common, even in buildings with security personnel.

4. When you leave your office, even briefly, keep the door locked.

5. When using an elevator, follow these procedures:

   a. If you find yourself waiting for an elevator with a suspicious-looking person, mutter something like "Oh, my mail," and head for the nearest safe area.

   b. Always stand near the control panel when you're in an elevator. If another passenger makes a menacing move, hit as many floor buttons as possible along with the alarm button.

   c. Make sure the elevator is going in the direction you intend. If you're going up, don't ever get into an elevator heading to the garage or basement, because attackers often lurk in these areas waiting for the elevator to deliver victims.

d. If your intuition tells you not to join someone who is already in the elevator, wait for the next car.

e. If you're already in and you feel frightened, push the button and get off at the next floor.

6. Avoid working in an office alone, especially at night. If you must do so, make sure the doors are locked, and don't open them for anyone you aren't expecting. Make sure someone knows you're there and checks in with you from time to time. Position yourself near a phone and have emergency phone numbers readily available. Know who else is in the building—co-workers and security personnel—and where they are, how to reach them, and what their schedules are.

7. As a condition of working at night, secure escort service to your car or public transportation. This is a valid request if you work in a neighborhood where the crime rate is high. In fact, ask for this service during the day if conditions indicate that you need protection.

8. Have a quick verbal response ready if you find yourself alone in an office with a potentially dangerous person. For example, if you've left the door unlocked by mistake and a suspicious-looking stranger comes in, say the following, without missing a beat: "Oh, I'm glad you finally got here. I expected you ten minutes ago. The other movers called from the corner, so they'll be here momentarily." If you're very convincing, the odds are he'll beat a hasty retreat.

9. Visit the restroom with a co-worker if you have any concern about possible assault. Your best protection is a company policy of keeping restrooms locked so that visitors to the building don't have easy access to them.

10. Know the neighborhood in which your office is located. Get to know the local police and security personnel, as well as the general crime situation in the vicinity. Ask for police or company security assistance in preventing incidents while you're in the building and nearby areas.

8 Travel Guidelines: Vacation and Hotel Security

If you're among the millions of Americans who are planning a trip, for either business or pleasure, the advice and tips in this section will be of particular interest. Recognize first that when you travel your ordinary routines are changed and you modify the ways you ordinarily behave. As a result, when you're away from home you may be especially vulnerable to crime and to people who prey upon travelers. You should make some special provisions—to protect both your home while you're away and yourself while you're in unfamiliar territory.

Preparing to Leave

The very best way to safeguard your home during any long absence is to have a "housesitter"—a close relative or trusted friend who will move in while you're gone. In most cases, however, this will not be possible, so here are a number of other suggestions to help disguise an extended absence.

1. Arrange for someone you trust to take care of your mail, newspapers, and any other deliveries, or suspend them for the duration.

2. Make sure your property will be kept up—lawn mowed in the summer, front walk and side walks shoveled in the winter—if you're going to be gone more than a week.

3. If possible, have a friend or neighbor stop by from time to time to readjust the blinds, turn lights on or off, and generally give your home the appearance of being occupied.

4. Install timing devices that will automatically turn strategically placed lights on and off after dark, including a bathroom light. You can control exterior lighting with either timing devices or "light-control sockets." The bulbs inserted into these sockets begin to glow as soon as it gets dark and become dim as the sun rises, even on a cloudy day. There are some limitations—for example, they don't work in smoked-glass fixtures—but they are effective in most circumstances.

5. Inform the local police of your intended absence so that they can check your property on their daily rounds, if you live in a residential area.

6. Be very discreet about your travel plans. There's no need to explain to vendors why you're suspending regular deliveries, or to announce to your dry cleaner (and anyone else who happens to be standing nearby) that you must have your clothes back by Thursday because you're leaving on Friday for a two-week vacation.

7. Ask a trusted friend or relative who knows your itinerary to call you in case of trouble. Post this person's name and number next to the phone so the police will know whom to contact.

8. Carefully check the references of anyone you hire as a professional housesitter, and don't consider anyone who doesn't have local references.

9. Be careful about packing your car. Whether you plan to use it during your trip or just to get to and from the airport or the train or bus station, place baggage, cameras, and whatever else you're taking just before departure, not the night before. It's much easier to break into a car than into a home.

While You're Away

While you're away, you should take the same precautions you would take at home. Perhaps most important is to be alert and aware, because vacation spots are considered lucrative territory by professional criminals. They know that travelers are on unfamiliar turf, often carry extra money, and tend to keep valuables in their rooms.

Here are some steps you can take in the handling of money while on a trip to minimize risk.

1. Carry as little cash as possible. Instead, take one widely accepted credit card (or, at the most, two), personal checks that can be cashed with your credit card, and travelers' checks. Be sure to keep the record of your travelers' checks in a safe place, separate from the checks themselves, so that you can report the numbers of missing checks and have them replaced in case of theft or loss. Each type of travelers' checks has different allow-

ances and procedures for replacing lost checks, and you should become familiar with these procedures.

2. Do not keep extra money in a suitcase. Divide your funds among family members (if applicable) so that all will not be lost if one of you is pickpocketed.

3. Exercise particular caution whenever you take out your wallet to pay for your hotel room, airline tickets, and other purchases. Many professional thieves "work" hotel and airline lobbies, watching potential victims to see how fat their wallets are and where they keep them. Be especially sensitive to anyone who "accidentally" bumps into you. If this occurs, check your wallet or purse immediately.

4. Carry your wallet deep inside your handbag or in a breast pocket—but absolutely not in your hip pocket, otherwise known as the sucker pocket.

Getting There and Back

For special precautions in using your car or on planes and trains, see Section 5, "Security in Your Car and on Public Transportation," earlier in this chapter.

Hotel Security

For most travelers, hotels or motels are homes away from home, but it's wise to remember that you'll be sharing this "home" with strangers. Thefts, robberies, and assaults sometimes occur, even in the best establishments. While these incidents are by no means common, and most hotels have security personnel whose job it is to look out for your well-being, the final responsibility for your safety and that of your property rests with you. To ensure a safe, pleasant stay, follow the precautions we recommend, and then go out and have a good time.

Watching Your Luggage

Both the street outside a large hotel and the lobby inside may be crowded, bustling places. The main area for you to be concerned about is the no-man's-land between the curb and the front desk.

1. Keep an eye on your baggage at all times, whether checking in or out. When you arrive, stay with your luggage until it is brought to the front desk. Don't just hop out of the taxi, bus, or limousine expecting that it will automatically be taken care of, and all you have to do is sign the register. Similarly, when checking out make sure that your bags are actually placed in the trunk of your car or in the loading bay of the airport bus or limousine.

2. Mark each of your bags—with a piece of tape on one corner, for example. Since many pieces of luggage look identical, marking yours will enable you to recognize them from a distance. Mark your hand luggage and attaché case in the same manner.

3. Use proper identification tags. The best kind does not have a transparent window, but encloses the identification card in a leather or fabric pocket. With this kind of a tag, someone can find out who you are and where you live without opening the bag if your luggage is lost, but this information isn't available to the casual—or not so casual—observer. If an airline requires ID tags that clearly show your name and address, it will provide these tags for each flight. Use them in conjunction with your own tags, but remove them as soon as you pick up your luggage in the baggage-claim area.

4. Mark your full name and address with indelible ink on the inside of each of your bags. This will help establish ownership in case someone else claims them.

5. Keep your luggage locked.

Registering at the Hotel
When you register in a hotel or motel, give only your last name and your first and/or middle initial. Don't give your first name, since it identifies your gender.

Maintaining Your Privacy
1. Be careful to divulge your whereabouts and plans only to those people who need to know. The information that you're from out of town, that you're staying in room 123 of the Such-and-Such Hotel, or that you plan to go on an all-day sightseeing trip the next morning can be valuable to someone who might be

planning to ransack your hotel room. So be sure to limit knowledge about yourself and your movements to people you trust.

2. Don't leave the hotel wearing a badge that gives your name, your business, and where you're staying if you're attending a convention. Put the badge in your pocket or purse until you return to the hotel. If you don't wear a badge, it will be assumed you know your way around the city; if you do, you identify yourself as a stranger and thus become somewhat vulnerable.

Storing Valuables

1. Put your valuables in the hotel vault; don't leave them in your room. This is one of the most important things to remember when staying at a hotel or motel. As soon as possible after checking in, take your extra cash, jewelry, and anything else you would be upset at losing to the front desk, and see that they are put in the vault. Get a receipt.

2. Take with you only the cash and travelers' checks you expect you'll need, plus one or two major credit cards, when you leave the hotel. Put the rest, along with a list of the numbers of the credit cards and travelers' checks you're taking with you, in the vault.

3. Don't try to outsmart thieves by hiding your valuables in your room. Professional burglars—including the few who may have conned their way into hotel employment—know every inch of the rooms they cover. They also know where people, even clever people, hide things, and they will be able to find whatever you try to hide.

Keeping Your Room Secure

1. When you're in your room, keep your door locked, using the deadbolt. If there is a chain lock, keep it attached, and twist the chain once or twice to reduce the slack, if possible. If for any reason your door won't close properly or the lock doesn't work, call the front desk and ask them to correct the problem at once or assign you another room.

2. If someone knocks on your door, make sure you know who it is and what his or her business is. If the person claims to be from

hotel maintenance or to be there to repair your television set or phone, don't open the door until you have called the front desk to make sure he or she is on legitimate business.

3. It's a good idea to take along a portable door-locking device, such as the Yale "Travelok," when you travel. Simple, compact, and very strong, this lock will fit just about any door or drawer. It consists of a locking plate, a locking bar, and a sliding lock, and adjusts to most standard locking configurations, making penetration difficult, if not impossible. It can be used as a backup device to prevent unauthorized entry, especially while you shower or sleep. If you use this or any other locking device on the inside of your door, leave the key inserted in it so that you can get out quickly in case of emergency.

4. Don't take your room key out of the hotel. Turn it in at the front desk, thus eliminating the possibility of losing it and having someone find it and clean out your room. If you lose your key, notify the hotel management immediately and ask to be transferred to another room.

5. Put the "Do Not Disturb" sign on the outer door handle except when you wish to have your room cleaned. This will give others the impression that the room is occupied. Leave the radio or TV set on when you go out, another indication that the room is occupied.

Taking Care in Hallways
Most hotel hallways are perfectly safe, but if you have any doubts at all, carry something at the ready. A whistle or shriek alarm will probably bring assistance, whereas yelling or screaming might be misinterpreted as the sounds of revelry or of a TV program.

An Ounce of Prevention
As we've mentioned before, security precautions are paid for by a certain amount of inconvenience. It takes effort to have your valuables put into the vault or to double-lock your door when you're tired after a late evening. But take the trouble—it's worth it.

Meeting Strangers

It's possible to meet many wonderful people while traveling, but you should keep in mind that there are some seemingly perfectly respectable people who specialize in victimizing travelers of both sexes. Be suspicious of any sudden interest—especially romantic interest—on the part of attractive strangers. Take your time and try to get to know them before you invite them up to "see your etchings." The most basic advice we can offer is "if in doubt, don't"—or even if *not* in doubt, don't.

Fire Precautions

Taking basic precautions in case of fire in a hotel can save your life. While most hotels are protected against fire, there are no guarantees. And hotel fires can be devastating because of panic among the guests, preventing them from making a safe and orderly exit. Here are a few simple guidelines:

1. Pack a small flashlight to keep by your bedside. A fire can knock out the hotel's electrical system.

2. Familiarize yourself with the basic plan of your floor.

3. Take the trouble to learn where the fire stairs or fire exits are located.

4. Check the exits to make sure they are usable. Do the doors open? Are the stairways clear?

5. Read the emergency instructions posted in your room, and if you have any further questions, contact the front desk.

6. In case of fire, take your room key and a wet towel, leaving as quickly as possible. Don't stop to gather other possessions. You will need your key if the only safe retreat is back in your room. Place the wet towel over your fact to reduce smoke inhalation.

7. Feel all doors before opening them. If the door is cool, open it slowly, with your shoulder propped against it so you can slam it easily if flames or heavy smoke are visible.

8. If the door to your room is warm or the hallway dense with smoke, stay in your room and seal spaces around the door with

wet towels. Use the phone to alert hotel personnel to your situation.

9. Avoid elevators and instead use fire emergency exits.

10. Review the information in Chapter Five on avoiding panic.

In the Vicinity of Your Hotel

Be especially cautious in exploring the area around your hotel. Even though you may feel at ease in the neighborhood after a day or so just because you're staying at the hotel, you should remain alert. Muggers like to work these districts, both the streets and the bars. They know how difficult it is for an out-of-towner to press charges should they be caught. Follow the precautions recommended in Section 4, "Street-Smart Behavior," earlier in this chapter.

Other Travel Tips

Parks and Wilderness Areas

If your travel plans include spending time in the great out-of-doors, you should still take measures against theft and assault.

1. Stick to designated camping areas.

2. Make sure to lock your car, camper, or motor home whenever you leave it.

3. Keep your campsite clean and orderly, and your possessions hidden from anyone casually strolling past.

4. Before going off by yourself for a hike or picnic, let the park rangers or park police know where you're going and when you expect to return.

Safety Abroad

Perhaps the most important thing to remember about traveling outside the United States is that you're not only visiting unfamiliar territory but also a different culture.

1. Do some research before the trip. Read about the country and talk to friends and acquaintances who have been there, as well

as to travel agents and the country's consular representatives in your home city.

2. Learn what you can about the local laws, appropriate dress and street behavior, and the crime situation in the places you plan to visit.

3. Turn to the United States embassy or consulate if you should need assistance during your stay. There are limits to what they can do, but they will make every effort to be helpful.

Chapter Two

In the Privacy of Your Home

There are many precautions you can take to remain safe and alive in the privacy of your home. Our focus in this chapter is on behavior that can reduce your vulnerability.

9 Basic Security Practices If You Live Alone

1. Be cautious about giving out your name, address, and phone number. See Section 2, "Restricting Personal Information," in Chapter One.

2. Conceal the fact that you live alone. For example, instead of putting your full name—Susie J. Smith—on the mailbox, write "S.J. Smith" to throw malefactors off the track. Or invent some roommates and list "S.J. Smith, P.D. Jones, G.J. Brown" on your mailbox, making it appear that more than one person is in residence. If you have a telephone-answering machine, your message might begin, *"We* are not able to come to the phone at the moment..."

3. It's safest to have an unlisted phone number.

4. The second-best method is a listing under your last name and first two initials. This reduces the risk of nuisance calls from people who skim through the telephone book looking for women to call and annoy.

5. If you must list your number, include only your name and number, omitting your address. If you are already listed and you wish to make changes, all you have to do is call your local telephone business office to make the necessary arrangements.

6. If you have plans to go out with friends, ask one of them to pick you up and return you to your door.

7. Date sensibly. More often than is generally acknowledged, a victim has been attacked by an acquaintance—not a stranger. Therefore, avoid situations at home (or in his home) in which you'll have to be alone with someone you don't know very well.

8. Take advantage of available escort services. These services are often offered to senior citizens who live in urban areas with high crime rates and to young women living on or near university campuses. Before using a privately run service in your community, check it out with the Better Business Bureau and ask for references from other clients.

9. Leave a radio on while you're out (or a radio, stereo, or TV if you're home) to give the impression of occupancy.

---

10 Safety at the Door

These precautions are valuable for everyone, but are especially important if you live alone.

When Arriving Home

1. Make sure the area near the entrance to your home is well lighted.

2. Don't enter alone if you have even the least suspicion that there might be trouble. Each time you arrive, check to see if the lock

has been tampered with or if the door has been forced or jammed. If everything looks all right but you still sense something is wrong or out of place, get help or call the police before you enter.

3. If you suspect someone is following you, don't enter your home. Head toward the nearest safety—a neighbor's house or apartment (if you're sure they're home) or a police station.

4. Have your keys out and ready so that you can enter quickly.

5. Bring groceries or bundles to the door before you unlock it. Too many people have developed the unsafe habit of unlocking their door and then carrying bundles, one at a time, from a car or elevator. This gives easy access to anyone lurking nearby.

6. If your home has more than one exit, make a bit of noise as you enter, giving a possible intruder a chance to get away. We suggest carrying on a conversation with an imaginary friend.

If You're Already Home

1. Don't open the door to strangers. That may sound ridiculously elementary, but people sometimes open the door rather than appear foolish or impolite.

2. Don't automatically feel safe if the person at the door is a woman. She could be part of a team or dangerous herself.

3. Don't open the door to casual acquaintances who arrive at your door uninvited. Too many women have been raped by such people to make this a safe practice. Tell the visitor that you're busy and would appreciate a phone call before further visits. No one has ever lost a friend worth having by setting these kinds of limits.

4. Always use your 180-degree peephole before opening your door. If you can't see the person, ask him or her to step back to improve your visibility. Maintain proper lighting in your entranceway, and keep spare bulbs handy.

5. If you live in a security building, don't buzz in anyone whom you don't expect or don't know. Since you can't see these people, you must be especially cautious. Refer them to the building manager if you have any suspicion.

6. Ask to see the credentials of maintenance, service, or delivery people—or even police. Check them through the peephole. If you didn't expect them, be doubly cautious. Call the building management, their place of business, or the local police precinct before allowing entry. Ask delivery people to slide the signature slip under your door. Sign it and return it in the same manner. Then direct them to leave the package by your door, and be sure they've left the premises before retrieving it. If you feel this isn't sufficient (for example, if there have been a number of recent incidents in the neighborhood), say that you'll pick up the package at the post office or the flowers at the florist.

7. Don't allow entry to strangers even if they sound frightened and in need of help. Speak to them through the door and provide assistance—for example, by making appropriate emergency phone calls—without opening yourself to risk. Following this admonition may be especially difficult on a cold or rainy night or if they announce they're being followed by someone dangerous. Be very careful—this could be a ruse.

8. Use your locks. Don't leave doors unlocked or open even if you are expecting a delivery.

9. Instruct household help and children—as well as all other adults in your family—to follow these same precautions.

---

11 Safe and Alive Telephone Practices

Here are some basic telephone safety habits or practices:

1. Tape the following numbers to each telephone in your home:
   Emergency Police or Sheriff's Department
   Fire Department
   Ambulance
   Paramedics (if this number is different)
   Family Doctor

Memorize the police emergency number so that you know it as well as the number of your best friend. Calling the police directly is usually faster than dialing "0" for the operator.

2. When making an emergency call, give your address first and then your name before stating your problem. If you're cut off, the police will know how to find you.

3. Consider installing a separate phone line in your bedroom. This gives you access to the police if a night intruder interferes with service on your primary line. Order a long cord for any bedroom phone so that, if necessary, you can take it into an adjacent bathroom that can be locked.

4. If you have a telephone-answering machine, be sure your message does not provide information that is useful to criminals. For example, don't say "I'm out now," but rather, "We can't come to the phone now." It gives the same basic message but does not reveal whether your home is empty, and therefore vulnerable. Again, using "we" instead of "I" indicates that more than one person lives on the premises. Omit your name from the announcement message to prevent others from looking up your address in the directory and burglarizing your home in your absence. If you're planning to purchase a new answering machine, buy one with a monitoring capacity so that you can screen your calls.

5. Don't give personal information to strangers who call, and instruct other family members and household help to be similarly discreet. Just because someone calls and announces in an official-sounding voice that he or she is taking a survey doesn't mean you have to participate. If you don't want to bother, simply say so and hang up the phone. If you do wish to participate, ask the caller's name, the name of the sponsoring institution or agency, and its phone number—and then return the call. If the survey taker balks at this procedure, hang up and forget it. Be especially suspicious of anyone claiming to be taking a survey of sexual attitudes or practices. These typically become obscene phone calls.

6. Don't let a stranger know that you are alone. If he or she wants to speak to your parents or husband or roommate, say that they are busy and will return the call as soon as possible.

7. If you receive a wrong-number call, don't give the caller your name or number. Instead, ask, "What number are you calling?" Tell these callers that they have reached an incorrect number or that there is no one by that name in this family. Then hang up.

8. If you place an advertisement in a newspaper or on a bulletin board, use your business phone, especially if you're a woman living alone. If that's impossible, ask a friend to screen the calls for you or temporarily hire the services of a professional answering service. Use only your last name and initials when placing such ads. See Section 9, "Basic Security Practices If You Live Alone," in this chapter for advice on how to list yourself in the telephone directory.

Dealing with the Telephone Intruder

Unfortunately, the telephone has become a useful tool to both pests and evildoers. Comedians make jokes about obscene or nuisance calls, but if you're on the receiving end they're not very funny. However, certain strategies reduce the likelihood of repeat calls.

1. Don't engage in conversation with strangers. We've said this before, but it's worth repeating. The obscene caller can be very clever. He might say something like "Steve gave me your number." Even if you have a friend named Steve, be sure there really is a mutual friend before responding.

2. If you receive a call that is obscene—even if it consists only of heavy breathing—say nothing and hang up immediately. If you have an answering machine, turn it on in case he calls back.

3. Keep a whistle or some other instrument that can make a loud, unpleasant noise by the phone. Once you're sure the call is obscene, blow it directly into the mouthpiece.

4. Call the phone company business office for assistance if the caller repeatedly harasses you. Obscene calls are felony offenses, but typically the police don't intervene until you have followed local phone company procedures. The people at the phone company are usually very sympathetic and will tell you what steps to take.

5. Consider changing your phone to an unlisted number if you are being harassed. We don't offer this as blanket advice, because psychiatrists suggest that, in rare cases, eliminating telephone access may push the caller into even more intrusive behavior. If you're in doubt, seek professional advice (see Chapter Seven).

---

12 Selecting Household Help and Providers of Services

The people who work for you—who babysit for your children, provide domestic services, repair your appliances, provide handyman's services or major home repairs—must be trustworthy. A few simple precautions when selecting and dealing with these people can help you avoid trouble later on.

1. Ask for a minimum of three local references and check them carefully. In addition to inquiring about the quality of the applicant's work, ask about his or her honesty. Was anything inexplicably missing? Was their home robbed while this person was in their employ or shortly thereafter? Were there any other unusual problems? If you receive troubling information, ask for additional references. You shouldn't hire the person if you detect any pattern suggesting possible criminal activity.

2. Get referrals from trusted friends and from service people with established excellent reputations. Such referrals are usually preferable to those from agencies or the Yellow Pages.

3. If possible, stay home with new domestic help or with repairmen and service personnel.

4. Return early the first few times you hire a new babysitter.

5. Ask a neighbor or friend to keep an eye on the house while the babysitter is there. Tell the sitter you have done so for her protection.

6. When workmen or service people are in your home, dress appropriately.

7. Repeatedly instruct babysitters and domestic help in basic safety guidelines to be followed while they are in your home.

8. If anyone commits a crime while in your employ, immediately report it to the proper authorities.

Chapter Three

Protecting Your Home and Car

Like charity, security begins at home. Whether you live in a mansion or an apartment, you should feel safe there. If your home has ever been broken into, if you've ever been robbed, if you've ever returned to find your place looking like a cyclone hit it, you know the difficulty of feeling safe again. A quiet sleep and sweet dreams are well worth the time and trouble spent on the precautionary measures that will help to keep you secure.

13 Thinking Like a Thief

In some communities the local police will, upon request, perform a security check of your home, advising you on how to correct weaknesses. The first step in securing your home is to get their professional opinion and follow their advice.

If you live in a community where this service is not offered, you can best assess your security needs objectively by thinking like a thief. You're smart, daring, resourceful, and wise to the ways people act and react. You're also in a hurry, and not likely to spend too much time (usually not more than four minutes) trying to break in. If it seems too difficult, you'll move on to an easier target.

Any potential burglar would attempt to answer the following questions:

1. *Is there anything worth stealing?*
What signs are there of wealth? Any high-priced cars in the garage or driveway? Expensive-looking paintings or sculpture visible through a window? Is this a neighborhood where people tend to have valuable possessions?

2. *Is the place occupied?*
Is there a car in the garage or driveway? Do piled-up newspapers or mail indicate that people are away on vacation? At night, do the same lights remain on hour after hour? Do any sounds, any radio or TV, indicate the presence of occupants?

3. *Can I get in easily?*
Are any doors or windows open or unlocked? Is a house key in some obvious location, such as under a doormat or flower pot? Do the doors and windows look sound? Can any be penetrated by breaking a single pane of glass? Are the locks new and sturdy or old and flimsy? How about the rear of the house or apartment? Would skylights, basement windows, or crawl spaces give me access? Are there indications that the home is protected by a professional security service? Can I get into an apartment through an adjoining apartment? Can I get into the garage?

4. *Am I likely to be seen by the neighbors?*
Does shrubbery shield me from passersby or people in nearby houses or apartments? At night, is there any outdoor lighting? Are there any "blind spots" where I can work without being seen? Are neighbors at home during the day? Are children playing in the vicinity? Are there indications of a neighborhood watch or a block association?

5. *Am I likely to be heard by the neighbors?*
Are the neighbors within earshot? Are alarm decals on the doors and windows? Is there a dog? If so, is it large and menacing or small and innocuous? Do the neighbors pay any attention to its barking?

6. *What tools or devices around the house will help me get in?*
   Is there a ladder lying around outside that can reach the second floor? Is one in an unlocked garage? Does a tree enable me to reach the roof or window? Does a fire escape allow easy entry? Are crowbars, hacksaws, gear pullers, hammers, or automobile jacks available in the garage or other outbuildings?

7. *When is the home most vulnerable?*
   Do the residents follow set patterns in their daily activities? Do they leave for work and return home at the same time each day? Do they usually work late? Do they go out the same evening each week? Do service people such as gardeners or delivery persons come at the same time each day or week? Is there a time when most of the neighbors are away at the same time— for example, on Sunday mornings when they go to church?

8. *What are my escape routes?*
   How do I get out of the house/apartment/neighborhood quickly in the event I'm surprised?

9. *How quickly do the police respond?*
   Is community police response swift or slow? Do police patrol the neighborhood on a regular basis? Are any private security patrols in evidence? Must I park so far away I'll get a double hernia carrying away the loot?

10. *What disguise, uniform, or diversion would throw the victim or neighbors off guard?*
    Can one deliver flowers without arousing suspicion? Are moving vans or U-Hauls frequently on the street? In an apartment building, can I pose as a maintenance or repair man?

---

14 Home-Protection Tactics

Once you've established the security weaknesses of your home from a thief's-eye view, you can take many precautions to minimize risk and impart the message that your home is not an easy target. Of course, your basic line of defense is a reliable and burglar-resistant set of locks aided by an alarm system, but before discussing them we offer some basic antiburglar advice.

1. Install outdoor lighting to illuminate your entranceway, garage area, or any place where a prowler could lurk undetected. If possible, install these lights high in the eaves of the roof to prevent tampering. Keep your house number lighted and clearly visible from the street so that the police, if called, can find the right place. Leave these lights on all night for best protection.

2. Close all blinds and curtains when darkness falls. This simple procedure prevents would-be intruders from figuring out who is or is not at home or gaining any other useful information about your habits. If you are home alone, you can disguise this fact by keeping the lights and/or radio on in another room.

3. If you go out for the evening, leave some lights and a radio on. Mechanical timing devices that turn your lights on and off in your absence are an extremely effective means of giving the appearance that the home is occupied. They are available at appliance and hardware stores. As you step out the door, call back to an imagined person inside the house "See you later—don't eat all the ice cream" or something of that nature.

4. If you live in an apartment, keep a spare lightbulb to replace any that burn out in your hallway or entranceway. If you return home and find your entranceway completely dark, don't enter your apartment alone.

5. Never publicize your absence by leaving a note on the door.

6. If possible, avoid regularly scheduled absences. Burglars can have a field day if they know that you are always out between certain hours.

7. All outside doors should be equipped with 180-degree safety viewers to enable you to see your caller without opening the door. Chain locks, unless they are unusually sturdy, can be easily broken.

8. Purchase a "Beware of Dog" sign and place it in a visible location even if you don't own a dog.

9. Place home-alarm-system decals at your front and rear entranceways and on windows. These may be available at your local hardware store. If not, have a printer make them for you.

10. If you have a garage, keep it locked at all times.

11. Ladders or other equipment that might be useful to an intruder should be kept under lock and key.

12. Develop a neighborhood watch or block association (more about this, Section 21).

13. Using an electric etching pen, place personalized identification numbers on your valuables. *Check with local police to determine the system of numbering they recommend.* Thieves know it's more difficult to fence stolen property that is so marked.

14. Carry insurance and document all your valuables, in case your home or apartment *is* burglarized. Make a complete inventory (we advise a written list and photographs) of all equipment, appliances, jewelry, silver, rugs, antiques, and anything else of value, including serial numbers. If possible, keep sales receipts with your inventory. Keep two copies of these records, at least one of them in a safe place away from your home. Most experts suggest keeping one copy in a bank safe-deposit box or with your attorney, accountant, a business manager, or a close relative. These records will provide the required documentation for insurance claims and will help police in tracing your property should that occur.

---

15 Doors, Keys, Windows, and Locks

There is no absolute guarantee against unwanted intrusion into your home. Nevertheless, the vast majority of burglars and other criminals can be deterred by properly secured windows and doors.

Doors

Doors require special attention because they are typically the easiest means of entering your home.

1. All exterior wooden doors should be solid core. Hollow-core doors are easy to penetrate.

2. Replace doors that have a good-sized window or, as an alternative, purchase bars for this window. Mail slots or other openings should be placed as far as possible from the latch.

3. Equip each exterior door with an 180-degree safety viewer or peephole.

4. Check each set of hinges to make sure it is properly installed. If these fasteners are not secure, a good push can dislodge them. If the hinge screws are too short, anyone with a pry bar can easily remove them. If you wish to make improvements yourself, we recommend the Time-Life book entitled *Home Security* for specifics on how to perform corrective surgery on problem doors (and windows, too). Otherwise, turn to a trusted friend who is handy or call in a reputable carpenter or handyman.

5. Secure sliding glass doors. These are especially vulnerable, but they can be made secure by placing a broom handle or wooden dowel in the bottom track and by driving a few flat pan-head screws into the upper track, making it impossible for anyone to remove the entire glass panel (see illustration). Glass doors may also be fitted with special bars and bolts. Try the Deerfield

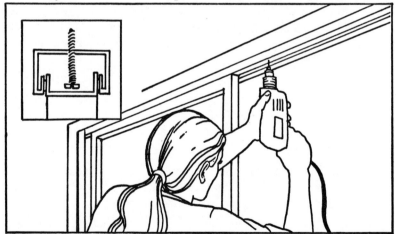

How to prevent a sliding door from being removed. Open the door and drill holes at ten-inch intervals in the overhead track with an 11/64-inch bit. Drive a 1½ inch No. 12 sheet-metal screw into each hole, allowing the screwheads to protrude enough to prevent the door from being lifted out of its tracks but not so far that they will rub the door as it is opened and closed (*inset*).

Lock Company of Deerfield, Illinois, for the latest in window and glass-door hardware.

6. Install a good set of burglarproof locks. See the section below devoted to this topic.

Keys

1. Take good care of your keys. Don't hand them out indiscriminately or leave them lying around so that they can be easily stolen.

2. Make sure your keys are not attached to anything with your name and address on it.

3. When you move into a new home or apartment, re-key your locks. You have no idea into whose hands the old keys may fall, so do this to be on the safe side.

4. Don't hide keys near the locks they open. Burglars are perfectly capable of checking under doormats or nearby flower pots. Don't underestimate them.

5. Select locks that require a special key that no ordinary locksmith can duplicate, such as Medeco or Ace locks. The only way you can get a replacement key is by writing to the manufacturer and sending proof of ownership (usually a copy of a registration card or original sales slip).

6. Consider a keyless electronic lock if you consistently lose keys. This type of lock operates by pushing a combination of buttons mounted outside your door. It is more expensive than a deadbolt, but is not much stronger. The main advantage is that you don't need a key.

7. Make sure that your car ignition key can be easily separated from your key ring. Don't leave your entire set of keys in the ignition when you park in a public lot.

Windows

There are a number of safety precautions and specific devices that can guard your windows against most intruders.

1. Outfit each window that has outside access with an appropriate type of lock. Secure double-hung windows with both a

butterfly latch and a nail (see illustration below). Use special window locks for sliding glass windows (see illustration on next page). These small devices, available at most hardware stores, screw into the track behind the window and are adjustable. With these locks, you can keep the window open slightly and still prevent anyone outside from sliding it all the way.

2. Replace louvered windows or guard them with metal bars because they are easy to penetrate.

3. Install laminated, tempered, or wired glass. Sheets of polycarbonate or acrylic plastic also offer extra protection, but they can cost as much as the special glass.

4. Install metal bars or grates if you feel you must. These are a very decorative and attractive deterrent, but they can represent a danger in the case of fire. If you install bars, we strongly

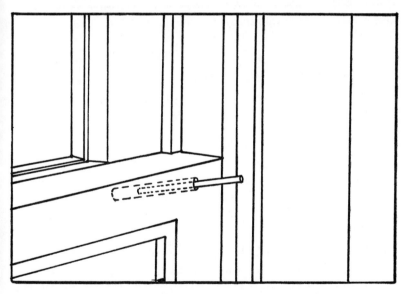

How to lock a window with a nail. Drill a 3/16-inch hole through the top rail of the bottom sash and into the bottom rail of the top sash. Angle the hole slightly downward so that the nail can't fall out if the window is rattled, and drill it at least ½ inch into the top sash. Trim the head from a 10-penny common nail with wire cutters so that the nail is just out of reach when it is in the hole. Keep a magnet near the window to retrieve the nail and unlock the window.

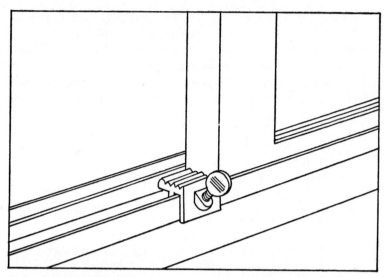

Lock sliding windows with special devices purchased at
the hardware store.

recommend that you purchase the kind with an emergency-
release feature. Teach all family members how to open them.

5. Key all window locks in a similar manner so one key can open
   them all. Keep copies of this key in handy locations.

Locks

1. Each door to the outside should have a spring-latch handle,
   ensuring that the door will automatically lock whenever it
   closes. This is your first line of defense, but it isn't adequate
   because professional burglars can open a spring-latch with a
   plastic credit card.

2. Install single- or double-cylinder deadbolt locks on all exterior
   doors. Deadbolts are constructed of solid brass, bronze, or
   stainless steel and, when installed, should extend at least one
   inch into the jamb. Single-cylinder deadbolts are operated by a
   key from the outside. The double-cylinder variety requires a
   key to get in or out, and it is ultimately sturdier. Also, if someone breaks into your home through a window, he won't be able
   to remove anything through the door. This feature won't protect cash, cameras, or jewelry, but it may make the removal of

larger possessions difficult or impossible. The main disadvantage of the double-cylinder deadbolt—and it is a considerable disadvantage—is that you must always leave the key in the inside lock when anyone is home to allow a speedy exit in case of fire or other emergency.

3. Install a Fox lock (sometimes called a police lock) if you live in a high-crime area. This lock consists of a metal bar braced between the door and the floor so that even if the lock is picked the door stays in place. It provides the ultimate in heavy-duty service.

4. Never depend on chain locks to provide total security. They tend to be flimsy and can be forced by anyone with superior physical strength.

5. Use the services of a professional locksmith for installation unless you are an experienced carpenter. Make sure the locksmith has an excellent reputation in the community and is properly licensed, and check to see that all employees are bonded.

6. Install locks on all bedroom and bathroom doors. These rooms can become sanctuaries if someone breaks into your home. If you can lock your bedroom and bathroom, the intruder may decide that breaking through isn't worth the effort. You may also gain a few extra minutes to call the police. If there are young children in your family, seek advice at the hardware store or from your locksmith concerning appropriate locks to install, and their placement.

7. Purchase only the most respected brand-name locks. Kahn, Emhart, Fichet, Medco, and Schlage are all widely recognized. What sets these locks above others is their construction. They are made of machine parts rather than cast parts and tend to last much longer. One locksmith told us he had seen Schlage locks that had been around for generations and were still in good condition.

8. Seek professional advice if you're not sure what kinds of locks are needed to protect your doors and windows. Local police or special community programs often offer this sort of consultation.

16 Alarm Systems

Simply defined, an alarm system is a device that, when activated, alerts you or someone else to an intrusion, fire, smoke, or other emergency. There are any number of different alarm systems on the market, ranging from simple devices sold at building-supply or hardware stores to state-of-the-art electronic or infrared systems that are custom-designed for the purchaser's specific needs.

These sophisticated systems offer just about anything a customer would want—wiring of windows and doors, electric eyes that trip when someone walks through them, pressure mats under the carpet, heat-sensing motion detectors, and closed-circuit TV banks monitoring activity at specified locations. Some are linked directly to the local police; others are connected by radio or telephone to a home-security company's central station, which alerts authorities if the alarm is tripped. Some make a racket when they go off (bells, sirens, horns, and buzzers are available); others are noiseless.

The current cost of installation for these kinds of systems begins at $2000 to $3000 and can easily run ten times these amounts. Customers pay monthly service fees for upkeep of the system and response in case of trouble. These fees are determined by the nature of the services provided.

Far less costly are devices you can install yourself. The most common are small self-contained battery-operated alarm units that provide spot protection at doors and windows. They make a loud noise when they're set off but can be deactivated quickly by an intruder after entry.

You can also install more complicated sound or vibration alarms that connect to an audio amplifier (similar to those used in stereo equipment) or that use vibration sensors. The main feature of these systems is their sensitivity. An intruder in sneakers will trigger the alarm. Unfortunately, pets can set them off just as easily, and even a curtain moving in a breeze can create enough vibration to set them off.

Before you decide on the type of system you need, keep the following in mind:

1. No burglar alarm is completely foolproof. Each system has at least one weakness or drawback. Professional burglars know this, because they spend time and money buying various commercial systems and figuring out how to beat them. However, most burglaries are committed by amateurs, so unless you've got very visible liquid assets, this isn't a serious problem.

2. Consider which areas most need protection. An alarm system can protect (a) the perimeter of your house (grounds or windows and doors), (b) a general area within your house, such as the basement, (c) a specific point, such as the cabinet housing your coin collection, or (d) a combination of the above.

3. Realistically assess what you have to protect, the crime situation in your neighborhood, and what you can afford.

Once you have decided on the type of system you need, follow these simple rules before committing yourself to buying from any alarm-system company:

1. Comparison-shop in order to get the most up-to-date merchandise at the best possible price. Get three or more bids on any alarm system.

2. Check with the Better Business Bureau to see if the company's record for service and performance is acceptable. Get references and check them out.

3. Make sure that employees of the alarm company are fidelity-bonded. This means that money has been pledged to ensure that the employees are honest.

4. Don't do business without a written proposal and a copy of the contract you'll be signing. Read these carefully. Don't sign unless all points of protection are listed and all the equipment to be installed is itemized. Don't sign if a lifetime guarantee is

offered—no such thing exists. If there is a monthly service fee, make sure this amount is cited in the contract along with the length of time before the fee is revised. If there is a charge for false alarms, make sure it's specified too.

5. Make sure you receive written instructions about how the system works and how to maintain it.

6. Be sure there is adequate provision for service and maintenance of the system. Without this, the quality of your protection will decline over time.

7. Keep quiet about your alarm system. Don't brag about how much it cost or how effective it is. The fewer people who know you have something valuable to protect, the better.

---

17 Professional Security Patrols

There simply aren't enough police to patrol constantly in residential neighborhoods and, because of governmental budget cuts, this situation isn't likely to improve in the near future.

As a result, a number of home-security companies offer residential security patrols as part of their services, and homeowners, especially in affluent neighborhoods, are glad to purchase this protection. It's our hunch that this service will become even more widely available in the future.

For about thirty-five to fifty dollars per month, homes are patrolled two or three times every twenty-four hours. Some companies offer guards who make perimeter searches every night, while others provide "drive-by" service.

Residential patrol guards drive radio-dispatched marked cars that can serve as a visual deterrent in the same way police cars do. Companies make an effort to assign guards regularly to the same neighborhood so they can spot anything out of the ordinary. In some instances, homeowners' associations hire the patrol, thereby decreasing the monthly cost for individual families.

18 Sentry Dogs

While it may be impractical or unsuitable for many people, owning a dog is an excellent deterrent to burglary or uninvited intrusion. Many dog owners find that their premises are untouched while their dogless neighbors are frequently victimized. Most thieves sizing up a property will avoid the complication of dealing with a dog and move on to an easier mark. Dogs are unpredictable, and no matter how gentle they may be as pets, most of them have an instinct for protecting their turf. However, significant differences in temperament make some dogs better watchdogs than others. A veterinarian can provide guidance on this issue, but some tips are worth noting here.

1. Look for the following qualities when selecting a puppy as a combination pet and protector:

   a. The puppy should come when called, with its tail up, and it should submit to handling after a brief period of struggle. Avoid the shy puppy who backs away or growls.

   b. Make sure the animal you choose has a strong, loud bark.

   c. Select an appropriate breed for your living space. Some types of dogs need more room and exercise than others. Consult a vet for advice on this matter.

2. Make sure you really want to own a dog. If you aren't particularly fond of dogs and you're considering one solely for security purposes, we advise you to find an alternative. Dogs require loving care, nutritious food, proper medical attention, and regular exercise and walking. They represent a major personal commitment.

3. Feed your dog in the morning rather than at night, as he will be more alert if he goes to bed a little hungry.

4. Provide obedience rather than attack training. If you feel your dog needs training to become a more effective protector, we

favor obedience training. (See Section 23 in Chapter Four for details.) Dogs trained to attack suspicious-looking people or any hand holding a weapon can turn on a guest or family member by mistake. These animals may be fine for police work, combat, or protecting commercial property, but they are risky as family pets.

5. Let your dog protect you away from home. If you jog, take your dog along. He will also enjoy an outing in the park, and you will benefit from his protection.

6. Install "Beware of Dog" signs near the front and back entrances of your home. These alone can provide some security.

---

19 Tools of Self-Protection

Our position regarding weapons and tools around the house was discussed in Chapter One. There is perhaps slightly more reason to keep weapons at home than to carry them around in public, but even this small advantage is offset by the potential risk that children will find a weapon and harm themselves or others. Further, if you take care to conceal a gun from a child, you might not be able to get it yourself in case of an emergency. It is legal to keep a gun at home, however, and if you do want to purchase one, we recommend a thorough and continuous course of instruction and practice (see Section 24 in Chapter Four).

Many objects around the house can be used for self-protection. In addition to all those that come quickly to mind—knives, chairs, liquor bottles, lamps, heavy-duty flashlights—consider the aerosal cans you might have in your kitchen or bathroom. Oven cleaner and deodorant sprays are useful to incapacitate someone temporarily; a small fire extinguisher is even more effective.

If you plan to throw something at an assailant, feint once before you actually throw it. If you throw it right away, his instinctive reaction may be keen enough for him to duck, but if you fake a first throw, he will think about it. The odds are that this will interfere with his basic instincts and that he won't be able to avoid the missile when you actually throw it.

Noisemakers can work at home as well as outside. If you have neighbors nearby, the sound of a bull horn or fire bell can alert them that you're in trouble, especially if you've informed them beforehand that you'll use these as a distress call. In addition, these sounds may startle intruders and cause them to beat a hasty retreat.

---

20 How Neighbors Can Help

We briefly discussed how neighbors can occasionally watch over your home in the section on travel and vacations. Neighbors can do much more than this, however; they can be a year-round deterrent to crime, as is being demonstrated on urban blocks and in suburban communities throughout the country. Listed below are the major ways neighborhood watch programs fight crime.

1. Neighbors can provide more or less continuous surveillance by being vigilant about activity in their area, by organizing shifts of local residents to walk or drive through the neighborhood at specified times, and by reporting all suspicious activity to local police authorities.

2. Neighbors can assist one another by sharing burglarproofing skills.

3. Residents can work with the local police to provide anticrime education and public-relations programs. They sometimes receive police training in surveillance and other crime-fighting tactics.

4. Finally, local residents can monitor the work of the police and the courts to make sure that their area is receiving adequate protection and that justice is being served.

Although there have been no comprehensive studies of community-based neighborhood-watch programs, police and residents in most areas feel they are effective. The major controversy about them is related to the hint of vigilantism inherent in some of their activities. In certain cases, these fears are well grounded, if the patrols carry weapons. However, armed citizen patrols are the exception rather than the rule.

On the whole, we're in favor of these programs and urge you to participate or to help get one started. If you don't have a neighborhood or community program, here are some basic steps in organizing:

1. Contact your local authorities for assistance.

2. Visit other programs in your area to see what does and doesn't work.

3. Form a committee of citizens interested in fighting crime in your neighborhood.

4. Set specific objectives and list the activities necessary to achieve them. Give special consideration to proven programs, such as neighborhood watch, court watching, crime prevention, seminars, and the like.

5. Organize your planning group, and othr ɔ in the neighborhood who will participate, into smaller subgroups to implement your plans.

6. Develop a realistic budget. If membership dues won't be sufficient, consider allying yourself with other organizations, such as YMCAs and YWCAs, churches, synagogues, or other reputable community groups.

7. Let the public, and especially the criminal element, know that your organization exists. You can publicize your group to the local media and through politicians. Bumper stickers and home decals are also effective.

There are secondary benefits to these kinds of programs. The organizational structure provides more community cohesiveness and less alienation. Through its collective voice, a neighborhood can be more effective in dealing with local politicians and bureaucrats.

---

21 Car-Protection Tactics

Stealing a car is often much easier than burglarizing a home. Whereas the house thief has to guess what (and who) is in the house, the car thief has only to walk up and look at the car to know that it's empty. At the same time, the car thief knows that most people are concerned only with their own cars. The neighbor of a person whose home is being burglarized might call the police, but the average person has less interest in the cars in his or her neighborhood. Thus the car thief can work almost with impunity.

Professional car thieves understandably favor the more expensive luxury cars, but no car, no matter how old or dilapidated, is safe from theft, and someone looking for a joy ride will select the first available vehicle. There is no sure way to prevent auto burglaries, but a number of precautionary measures can help.

1. Don't leave your keys in the ignition. It has been estimated that more than half of the car thefts in the United States happen because keys are left in the ignition. Take your keys with you, and always lock the car when you leave it. Make this a habit.

2. Keep your ignition key on a separate key chain, not with your house and/or office keys. If an unscrupulous parking-lot attendant has both your car and house keys, he can have the house keys copied, trace your address through your license-plate number, and use the keys to burglarize your home.

3. Keep your trunk key separate from your ignition key. That way, if you park in a commercial lot, the contents of your trunk will be comparatively secure.

4. Keep a spare set of car keys with you. If you lose one set or lock yourself out of your car, you'll be able to get going much more quickly and cheaply.

5. The best place to leave a car is in a locked garage. The car itself should be locked, and the garage lock should require a key to open it from both the inside and outside. Garage windows, too, should be securely locked.

6. Never leave valuables in the passenger compartment. Keep all packages locked in the trunk.

7. Don't depend solely on auto burglar alarms. Once people install these devices in their cars, they tend to ignore some of the foregoing safety measures. And, since many auto alarms go off for no apparent reason, neighbors and passersby treat them more as a nuisance than an indication of trouble.

Chapter Four

Getting
Special Instruction

Fortunately, even if your immediate neighborhood has no organized watch program, local communities provide many protective services. Some of this assistance falls into the category of free or low-fee courses in various defenses, often sponsored by local law-enforcement authorities or by community organizations with anticrime programs. Instruction is generally available in self-defense and physical fitness, canine obedience training, the handling of weapons, and home-security techniques.

22 Self-Defense and Physical-Fitness Classes

Choosing self-defense classes is somewhat like choosing a mate—you have to go with what feel best for you rather than with what someone tells you. There are too many different martial arts and systems of self-protective instruction to describe here, but we can offer the following guidelines.

1. Shop around—visit various self-defense studios. Call ahead

and ask permission to watch a class (some places permit visitors only at specified times).

2. Observe the instructor closely as he or she teaches, and watch the students as they respond. By visiting a few places, you can gain a clear idea of the style of self-defense you like best. Then determine which teacher impresses you as being most competent. You should also feel comfortable with this person, as your rapport with the instructor is a key factor in choosing the right course. Let this sense, rather than any high-sounding credentials, be your guide, and don't worry about whether the instructor is the same sex as you are.

3. Be ready to make a serious commitment to learning. This will involve practicing at least twice a week for three months. If you can't make that commitment, it's probably better to wait until you are sufficiently determined.

We recommend classes in physical fitness, especially if you're out of shape. People in good physical condition have greater self-confidence and simply do not look like potential victims. Not only are they better able to flee from danger, but they are better able to withstand physical attack. As with self-defense classes, you are faced with a dizzying array of possibilities. We advise you to use the same criteria as when selecting self-defense instruction.

---

23 Canine Training

We don't recommend attack training for family pets. The risk of accidental injury to family members and friends outweighs any security benefits. Instead, we favor obedience lessons followed by protection training. Your dog can then provide valuable security for your home and family without sacrificing the companionable, reliable qualities that have endeared him to you as a pet.

1. *Obedience training.* The purpose is to teach the dog to obey the simple commands of family members. Classes run eight to ten weeks, and a family member participates with the animal. The dog learns to sit, lie down, come when called, and heel. Most trainers agree that the majority of household pets can learn to obey these commands, especially if they begin obedience training at an early age—from four months onward. Dogs must complete the course successfully before starting protection training.

2. *Protection training.* An initial purpose of this kind of instruction is to teach your dog to bark frantically at any stranger. Of course, many pets do this habitually without being trained to do so. You can also train the family pooch to become a "threat dog" who will appear menacing on command. On signal, the dog will adopt a watchful, alert stance, and on further command he will bark loudly and snarl menacingly. Your dog need not be a large or aggressive breed; he must merely be trainable to the extent that he can quickly appear threatening. As with obedience training, dogs learn best if instruction begins when they are young.

If you're absolutely convinced that you need an attack dog, experts recommend the Schutzhund program of training, originated in Germany. The dog is taught to bite on command through the repetition of ego-building games in which he is amply rewarded for the "right" action. These programs also include instruction in retrieving and tracking.

Choosing a Good Trainer

Since there is little in the way of formal licensing or professional regulation for dog trainers, you should seek references for good trainers from leading dog clubs and associations in your area. These groups are usually organized by people who love, own, and breed dogs and who have an interest in seeing that their animals are well trained. Veterinarians are also good referral sources.

When selecting a trainer, look for the following kind of person:

1. Someone who is willing to discuss his or her teaching methods and philosophy. You should be comfortable with both.

2. Someone who will take the time to discuss what you consider the specific needs of your family and your situation.

3. Someone who will test the personality of your dog on an individual basis before training begins. Specific "courage" tests can weed out potentially dangerous or unpredictable animals.

4. Someone who will involve you or another family member in the training. After all, the trainer won't be there after the classes are over.

---

24 Handling Weapons

In Chapter One we expressed our disapproval of the firearm as a reliable means of self-protection. Except in rare and unusual circumstances, the disadvantages of firearms far exceed the benefits. If, however, you do plan to buy a gun, or if you already own one, we urge you to seek instruction in both firearm safety and marksmanship. This training should not be undertaken lightly; you will be learning a skill that, if applied incorrectly, could have dire physical, legal, emotional, and ethical consequences.

Becoming thoroughly competent in the use of arms requires a substantial commitment—many hours of practice and of familiarizing yourself with your weapon. It's important, too, that you become aware of when it is or is not appropriate to use such force. If you keep a gun in the house just to feel safe, you pose a potential danger to both yourself and others.

Information about firearm safety and marksmanship is available from the Clubs and Associations Department of the National Rifle Association, 1600 Rhode Island Avenue N.W., Washington, D.C. 20036. Write them for the name and address of the NRA-affiliated marksmanship club nearest you, and then contact the club to find out if it is qualified to give instruction in home firearm safety as well as in marksmanship. The

NRA has been giving small-arms instruction for well over a hundred years.

After you have completed your markmanship instruction, be sure to continue practicing on a regular basis (at least monthly) at a local firing range. Learn the local statutes governing self-defense and gun use, and continually remind yourself of the ethical responsibility to use weapons only to save life. Finally, we urge you again not to depend on the firearm; depend instead on your vigilance, your intuition, and on all the other self-protective measures at your command.

Tear Gas

We have similar reservations about the effectiveness of tear gas in self-defense. We do not believe that the standard three-hour course of instruction is sufficient time in which to become competent in the rapid and proper deployment of this chemical spray against a determined aggressor. If you take tear-gas instruction, you should follow it up with additional training (perhaps in the martial arts) in order to develop the mental control and protective responses necessary to use the device effectively in situations of high stress and rapid movement. This training should also prepare you to take action in case the device malfunctions or the chemical is ineffective.

You should also investigate local and federal laws governing private use of tear gas. In most states you must be licensed to carry this weapon, and there are some restrictions concerning its possession (for example, on commercial airlines).

---

25 Home Security Checks

In many communities the police or others working in crime-prevention projects will visit your home to assess how safe and secure it is from intruders. They will then make specific suggestions for improvements.

These services are most readily available to senior citizens and to residents in smaller towns or cities. Sometimes this assistance is available through neighborhood-watch programs. We urge you to take advantage of these programs, checking first, of course, to make sure that the sponsoring organizations are reputable.

If no such program exists, you might ask a friend or relative who is sophisticated in such matters to walk through and around your home in order to check the following:

1. Doors

2. Windows

3. Locks

4. Exterior lighting

5. The garage

6. The zone between the place where you park and your front or back door, or

7. The entrance to your apartment building and your front door

If there are problems, sit down with this person and work out solutions. If you don't have the available cash, perhaps a local locksmith will do some work for you in exchange for some service you can render. Perhaps a handyman or woman will do some work for you if you can arrange for a story in your local newspaper that will publicize his or her business. Perhaps tenants in your building can share skills. There are many possibilities.

Part Two

Preparedness: When Prevention Isn't Enough

No matter how cautious or sensible you are, you can find yourself in a dangerous situation or the victim of a violent crime. Since there are clear and specific means by which anyone can prepare for such eventualities, Part II of this book is devoted to this general topic.

There are two compelling reasons why preparation is worth your time and energy. First, you can reduce the likelihood of being physically harmed, or you can at least reduce the degree of harm. Second, preparation brings with it some potentially positive psychological side effects. Now only will you feel less like a victim and more in control, even in threatening circumstances, but you'll be able to help others who need assistance.

As part of our discussion, we will introduce some of the basic principles of Aikido, the nonviolent Japanese martial art. We recognize that some of these principles or practices are best understood by observation or participation rather than through the written word, and we therefore urge you to visit a *dojo* (where Aikido is taught) in your community to observe a class in action. Watching a class will make some of this material come alive in a more meaningful manner.

Chapter Five

Reducing the Risk of Harm

You can't prepare for the possibility of a crime in the same way you can rehearse a staged scenario, where action and dialogue are spelled out in detail. In any real-life drama of danger, the only person whose behavior you can control is your own. If you can avoid panic and remain clearheaded, calm, and aware of the probable consequences of your actions, you can significantly reduce your chances of harm.

26 Gaining and Regaining Your Composure

There are two main guidelines to help you to become calm and alert.

First, accept the fact that you may not be able to control your initial response. If, for example, another car cuts you off while you're driving and you manage to avoid an accident by inches, chances are the adrenalin will pump through your body, causing you to feel rage or extreme physical discomfort for a few seconds. Similarly, if you come face to face with a dangerous or threatening person, your bodily defenses may automatically spring into operation. Accept this initial reaction, whatever form it takes, because it is your body's primitive means of protecting you. Don't be alarmed by or resist this reaction. It will pass quickly if you accept that it's there in your service.

Second, use centering techniques. "Centering" is a process used in Aikido and other martial disciplines, and it is applicable in everyday situations. It is a way to unify body, mind, spirit, awareness, and intentions. This unification brings you to a state of balance and readiness in which you function at peak efficiency, always choosing the most appropriate response to the situation confronting you. You are both clearheaded and decisive. You know what must be done or said, and you set about it at just the right time.

When you are not centered—that is, when you are unaware or out of sorts—you tend to respond to fearful situations by either freezing or reacting impulsively without using the full force of your intelligence. You can accomplish the transformation from being uncentered to being centered virtually instantaneously.

For thousands of years, Oriental warriors have studied the basics of human balance. According to their collective wisdom, surviving an attack by a trained and determined opponent depends on one's ability to meet the attack in a balanced, relaxed, alert, and agile manner. The key to reaching this state, they believe, is an awareness of one's center, an imaginary balance point located about two inches below the navel and two inches in. The Japanese consider this point the center of a person's being, a boundless reservoir of calm and tranquility, a mirror-flat lake, a place beyond space and time. We sometimes refer to it as "the pit of the stomach" or the place where "gut reactions" originate. Never mind that your center doesn't exist on any anatomical charts in any medical school.

To become centered, follow these steps:

1. *Imagine that your center of gravity sits below your navel.* Try to visualize this spot. Let all weight and heaviness, all tension and fear sink down into your center. Whatever it is that frightens you, take it and push it down into this bottomless drain. Do not

give up on this process. No matter how afraid you may be, continue to draw your fear downward into your center. Soon you'll be able to master your fear, so don't stop until you feel balanced and calm, until your center of gravity is low. Breathing deeply facilitates this process.

2. *Straighten your back.* Let your spine straighten slightly. Don't force it into a military posture, but straighten it nonetheless. Let your head float on your neck, but remain levelheaded.

3. *Relax.* Let your shoulders soften and round slightly, while still keeping your spine straight. Let your jaw fall slightly so that your mouth is just a bit open. Tell yourself silently to relax. The more you relax, the more easily you'll choose the right course of action and the more energy you'll have for possible use later on.

4. *Practice these techniques.* Practice them in everyday situations of tension—for example, when you're angry with someone you love or with your boss, when you're feeling frustrated while waiting in line or on hold on the telephone. The more you practice centering, the more it will become second nature.

5. *Control feelings of panic.* Panic is a fear that can become all-encompassing. It drives people beyond reason and logic, often sending them right into the very danger (fire, for example) they are trying to escape. In disturbances in public places, people will often rush for the exits only to be crushed to death by other crazed persons. It usually turns out that if they had remained calm, no one would have been hurt. If you find yourself in imminent danger and start to feel panicky, center and then say to yourself—over and over if necessary—"Panic is my worst enemy." Regain a state of relative calm, and then decide which of the responses described in Chapter Six is most appropriate.

6. *Use memory and visualization techniques.* Another means of calming yourself in situations of danger is to recall and visualize those moments in your past when you felt completely tranquil and safe. Your mind can function like a computer, retrieving such moments so you can recapture that sense of peace and bring it into a present situation. Again, practice in doing this will be helpful.

7. *Think about your loved ones.* Many people are able to get through very difficult situations by thinking not of themselves but of their children or spouse or someone else who depends on them. If you have a strong instinct to protect and care for others, remembering those who depend on you can be calming in dangerous situations.

---

27 Following Your Intuition

Once you are centered and calm, allow yourself to act spontaneously. Don't try to appraise the situation logically, just react from your gut. It's very easy to do, actually, but it means you must trust—in God, in yourself, in the universe, in something that works for you.

Your intuition—your capacity for spontaneous insight—is one of your greatest assets. This innate ability to simultaneously see, choose, and act is probably the single most important survival mechanism you have. Your intuition tells you, independent of logic or reasoning process, which is best among the many choices you have in a given situation. It does so instantly, and it is never wrong. More than that, intuition can often be shown by hindsight to have played a critical part in saving you from a dangerous or difficult situation of which you were unaware at the time.

The times you're most likely to operate intuitively are when you're relaxed, aware, and yet slightly detached from what's going on around you. In this state of comparative calm, you can sense a phony despite the most clever disguise.

1. Trust your intuition. Don't deny its power and don't ignore its signals. Be ready to do what it tells you, regardless of the logic involved.

2. Be aware of your response patterns. Patterned responses are the chief enemies of intuition. Challenge your basic assumptions about people or situations. Just because a man is dressed as a priest doesn't mean he *is* a priest. Just because the bank

looks quiet from the outside doesn't mean it's not being robbed. Professional criminals study how we react to other people and use this information to prey on us. They know, for example, that our image of a burglar is an unshaven thug wearing shabby workclothes, so they dress like IBM executives. This doesn't mean you should be chronically suspicious, but that you should let your intuition be your guide.

---

28 Evaluating Your Strengths, Correcting Your Weaknesses

Chances are you've already survived a number of difficult situations. If you think about those incidents, certain patterns should emerge. Perhaps you talked or joked your way out, or maybe you ran like an Olympic sprinter.

Look at your past survival strategies to get a sense of your strengths and weaknesses, and read the next chapter, which discusses possible options for response, to bring this into even clearer focus.

Should you discover that you lose your voice in times of stress or that running away from danger would be difficult because you're very out of shape, you can do something about this. Classes in everything from self-defense and physical fitness to assertiveness training can help you to enlarge the variety of options at your disposal.

---

29 Planning Specific Responses

Even though each encounter with a criminal is unique, you can consider beforehand what your responses should be to specific situations. For example, if someone approaches you on a deserted street with a gun or knife and tells you it's your money or your life, a quick evaluation of your priorities should indicate that your personal safety is worth much more than anything you possess. We also advise planning for such eventualities so that anger or some primitive instinct won't take over. A tug-of-war with a mugger can end in tragedy.

Throughout the book you'll find many examples of possible responses—for example, what you might say to avoid joining a suspicious person on an elevator, what you might say to a stranger at the door or to someone entering your office while you're working at night. You can practice these responses until they become your own words.

With your family or a group of friends, you can invent and practice appropriate and life-saving responses. Take notes during such discussions so you can reflect on the best ideas afterward. The primary purpose of preparation is to enable you to select the most appropriate and life-sustaining option in the event of danger.

Chapter Six

Options for Response

In even the most critical situation involving imminent danger, you have an array of available responses. In this chapter we will describe these choices and suggest some guidelines for selecting the ones that will be most appropriate in specific kinds of encounters.

Although each of these responses is best defined operationally, according to the specifics of a particular situation, some general differences are worth noting.

1. *Fighting.* This involves resistance using physical force (with or without weapons) in response to an unprovoked attack.

2. *Flight.* Defined most simply, this means escape or evasive action taken to separate you from your attacker; it includes hiding.

3. *Negotiation.* Dialogue opened by you with your attacker for the purpose of forestalling an attack or of reducing its harmful effects through bargaining.

4. *No action.* This literally means doing nothing to change the situation—that is, carrying on as though nothing unusual is happening.

5. *Surprise or diversion.* These are actions taken in order to confuse, mislead, or startle your assailant.

6. *Blending.* Joining temporarily with your attacker's force to re-direct it and eventually gain control. This Aikido concept can be understood most readily through a simple experiment:

a. Insert the index finger of your right hand into the fist of your left hand. Reverse procedure if you are left-handed.

b. Hold the finger very tightly so you can't pull it away.

c. Resisting with your clenched left hand as hard as you can, try to pull the finger away. It should be impossible to do so.

d. Now, very quickly, thrust the squeezed finger in the direction it's being held and then immediately pull it away. This should be easy to do.

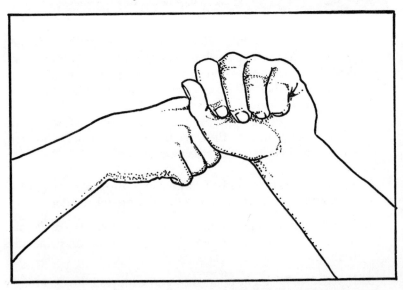

Try this experiment with another person to get a sense of what it's like to be held against your will and then to free yourself.

Blending is not a party trick in which you are successful merely because of the element of surprise. Prove this to yourself by doing the exercise repeatedly. The same liberating result always occurs.

What's happening is that you temporarily (for a split second in the finger experiment) join with your attacker's force, momentum, or design for the purpose of eventual control and redirection. Blending may at times appear to be surrender, but it never is. Those who use blending strategies are really only biding their time.

None of the responses discussed in detail below is either good or bad, right or wrong, except as it proves effective or ineffective as a means of removing you from danger. Each situation is unique, calling for its own individual solution. One incident might require you to fight for your life; another might demand that you run for it. There are times when you may be able to talk your way out of a jam, and sometimes the best thing you can do is keep your mouth shut. The important thing is to choose the appropriate option, the one that brings you out of danger safe and alive.

---

30 The Fight Option

We hope you will never have to fight another person to defend your life. It can be a terrifying experience. But if you ever *are* the victim of serious, unprovoked physical assault, know that your attitude or spirit—more than your size—is the determining factor in pulling you through. If you are paralyzed by terror or fragmented by the sudden assault, you lose what is most commonly called "a fighting chance." If, on the other hand, you are able to unify yourself—collecting your wits, muscles, and soul and fusing them into an all-out drive for survival—you will prevail.

Prepare yourself for this unification by recognizing that the fight option is based on the following assumptions:

1. *You have the right to life.* Self-preservation is the very first and most fundamental law for all living things. This right sanctions your own will to live and is your primary asset.

2. *There are no rules.* This is not a contest, like a prizefight or a football game. By attacking you, your assailant has broken both the law of the land and the bonds of basic human trust. To

survive his attack, to immobilize or escape it, you must be prepared to break all rules, restraints, and conventions. Do what must be done to save your life, no matter how unfair or unethical such measures might be under ordinary circumstances. Prepare yourself to use any means possible to ensure your attacker's capitulation or retreat, but use no more force than is absolutely necessary to achieve these ends.

3. *Fight forward, not back.* This suggests both a psychological attitude and a physical stance. "Fighting back" implies that the attacker has the initiative and that you are seeking revenge. This must not happen. You must be prepared to take the lead immediately—not by striking back at your assailant, but by driving forward through him as if you were charging through an open door. You must be filled with righteous anger, using it to protect both yourself and your attacker. Beyond saving your life, you are possibly minimizing the consequences he would face were you to be mortally wounded.

4. *Size and strength don't matter.* In a life-threatening situation (one in which no rules apply), size and strength are not very important. Size and strength matter in competition, where rules and fair play are paramount; but where your survival is at stake, they are only two attributes out of many that could save your life. The main weapons in mortal combat are sincerity, determination, and an indomitable spirit. Focus your energies and you will generate a force of overwhelming, incomprehensible physical power, one that dwarfs the mere muscles of the strongest man.

You have probably heard or read accounts of people saving their own or others' lives against odds that seemed impossible. For example, the *Los Angeles Times* recently reported an incident in which a man lifted a fallen telephone pole that was about to crush a child. He was amazed to learn later that the pole weighed over a thousand pounds. This life force—in service to oneself or others—is truly amazing.

When to Fight

Although every situation has its own specific variables, the most appropriate times to use the fight option are:

1. When a sudden, unprovoked attack is made on you at close quarters and you feel in imminent danger of bodily harm. This assumes that the option of flight is less attractive.

2. When the situation is worsening, even though you may not yet be under direct attack. When fighting now will prevent you from having to fight later from a less advantageous position, you had better begin. If someone who is intent on killing you pushes you into a room and turns to lock the door, don't wait until he has finished the job. Start your attack immediately.

3. When someone's life is in imminent danger and your immediate and forceful intervention is vital.

How to Fight

Let's assume you are attacked: without provocation, someone suddenly assaults you. The situation is critical. Keep the following in mind:

1. Concentrate your force. Center yourself (see the discussion of centering in Chapter Five), keeping your knees slightly bent and springy and your center of gravity low. Take as deep a breath as time allows.

2. Assess your assailant's weaknesses if time permits. (If there is no time, move directly to step 3.) His weaknesses may be physical, mental, or emotional. Something about the situation (the shape of the room, for example, or the fact a police car has just turned the corner) may put him at a disadvantage. Exploit this opportunity quickly.

3. Fight forward fast. Whatever your physical condition, use the following sequence:

    a. Imagine a small open window located right smack in the middle of your attacker's chest. If your attacker is very tall and you aren't, imagine this window located in his abdomen, slightly below his navel.

    b. Screaming like a seahawk, use every ounce of your strength, guts, and sheer willpower to drive your body right through this window and out the other side of his body. Don't worry about how to do this; simply rip, tear, claw, gouge, bite, and

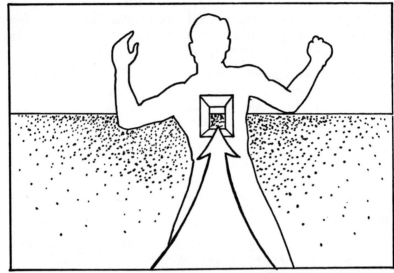

kick your way through every one of his defenses. Squirm, twist, weave, bob, and zigzag past any attempt to stop you. Use any weapon or ally the situation provides. Above all, refuse to be denied.

c. Don't stop until your assailant has abandoned all resistance and is either immobilized or running away. Don't try to escape until you have made sure your attacker is incapable of following you and attacking you from behind.

Where to Fight

The best place to fight is in a street or some other public place where the chances of your being seen, heard, and assisted are comparatively high. Failing that, fight anywhere.

Whom Not to Fight

Some attackers are more difficult to deal with than others, and it is better not to fight them. Among them are the following:

1. Someone who is suicidal or who believes he has nothing to lose.

2. Someone who is mentally deranged, whether the derangement is chronic or temporary, as a result of alcohol or drugs, especially Phencyclidine (PCP).

3. Multiple attackers—people in groups or gangs.

4. Someone who *threatens* violence against a helpless person in your care, such as an infant, an invalid, or an elderly person.

5. Someone who fanatically believes that his or her attack is a righteous act—for example, a political terrorist.

When Not to Fight
It's wise not to fight in the following circumstances:

1. When there's a chance you can escape.

2. When you can persuade your assailant to stop the attack.

3. When your attacker(s) have firearms or other weapons and you believe they will use them at the slightest sign of noncompliance.

4. When you believe that help is coming and you can stall or divert your assailant.

---

31 The Flight Option

Running for your life requires just as much preparation as fighting. Immediately, within a split second, drop whatever you're carrying, pick up your feet, choose your direction, and sprint!

Fleeing to save your life is not, in itself, a cowardly act. If you're walking down a street and hear what sounds like shots, take cover. If it's only a backfire, the worst you will face is amused embarrassment. So what if you overestimate the danger? It shows you're alert, prepared, and that you value yourself and your life.

If you choose to run for cover, keep in mind that hiding is an inferior form of flight unless the surrounding area offers many places of concealment. Hide in the place that is least likely to be searched. Once hidden, concentrate on anything but your pursuers. They may be drawn to you by the very force of your fear.

When to Flee

Following are some suggestions on when to flee. Although they may seem obvious, a review is helpful.

1. The best time to run is as soon as you safely can. The moment you sense a situation is getting out of hand—someone is becoming violent, uncontrollably hostile, or abusive—get away fast. Waiting increases your involvement and decreases your chances for escape. Delay is wise only if an early escape attempt clearly risks your being caught.

2. Leave the scene when you're in a crowd that suddenly gets aroused or upset. Move quickly to the fringes of the crowd, at a right angle to the focus of interest. Move laterally and in a crouching posture so that you stay below the crowd's normal line of vision. Don't push or jostle anyone, but slip and slide around them while repeating "Excuse me, please" or "I'm sorry" in a nonthreatening, conciliatory tone.

3. Make an escape when your attackers or captors drop their guard and you feel there's a good chance you can get away. Be ready to capitalize on their mistakes. Think beforehand about the conditions necessary for successful escape and the nearest place of sanctuary.

How to Run Away

Fleeing an attacker isn't always a matter of merely running as fast as you can. Following are some tips to keep in mind.

1. Run toward safety, not away from danger. There's a right way and a wrong way to escape. The wrong way is to panic, which will draw pursuit, much as running from a dog will incite it to attack. The right way is to run *toward* someplace, which makes it a positive action. You're not running away; you're just advancing in reverse.

2. Don't hesitate once you've decided to run. Go for daylight, and don't stop until you're certain you're free and clear.

3. In close quarters (for example, inside a house), resist the temptation to run at full speed. If you're in a strange house, or some other confined space, you could run into something and hurt yourself badly, making it easier for your pursuer to catch you. Keep your speed down until you have a clear field.

4. It may be advisable to take off your shoes if the terrain and the climate permit it. Running in bare feet gets you over a lot more ground than running in uncomfortable shoes. It's also quieter.

5. Put obstacles between you and your pursuer. In a room, pull over chairs and tables. On the street, dodge around parked cars, pull over garbage cans, run through traffic, do whatever you can to tire your pursuers. These precious seconds and minutes are in your favor, and weaken the attacker's will to pursue.

6. Put money between you and your pursuer. Throw down bills if you have them, coins if you don't. We're so attracted to money in our culture that it takes a strong will not to pick up tinkling coins or fluttering bills. Jettisoning your cash at just the right time may break your assailant's train of commitment, forcing a choice between you and the money.

7. Think while you run. Look ahead to your destination, perhaps a police or fire station, a hospital, a hotel lobby, the home of a friend or relative. Are they likely to be there? Can they help you? How far away are they? What's the best route? Is there a backup if the first idea doesn't work? Keep thinking; keep running. As the great baseball player Satchel Paige said: "Don't look back."

Whom to Run From

Typically, the people to run from are those whom it would be most difficult to fight. If they believe they have nothing to lose, if they are deranged, or if they are fanatically committed to a cause, they are the most dangerous. It's also wise to separate yourself from agitated people who think they're defending their territory against an intruder, which may make them especially violent. Get away fast.

---

32 The Negotiation Option

For our purpose, negotiation means opening a dialogue between you and the attacker, the goal of which is to persuade him to terminate his attack, modify it, or minimize its harmful effects upon you.

Negotiation can be difficult in a fast-moving encounter. People under the influence of alcohol or drugs may not be able to understand anything you say to them, nor is a professional criminal likely to let you persuade him to change his way of life. But sometimes people can negotiate to bring about less disastrous results than would otherwise occur. A man who is being mugged, for example, may be able to talk his mugger into leaving him his personal papers and family photographs. A rape victim may persuade the attacker to put his weapon down and to allow her to take contraceptive measures. Compared to the enormity of the crime, these may seem like small advantages, but they're actually quite important. By persuading your attacker, or by attempting to do so, you've demonstrated that you're not a victim, that you've tried to do something to change the situation in your favor. You haven't stood by mutely and cooperated in your own victimization.

Even if you're unable to win any concessions, negotiation can win you time. The longer you keep your assailant talking or listening to you, the more controlled affinity you can foster. The more affinity, the less likely you are to be harmed and the more the situation is likely to change in your favor. If your assailant refuses to negotiate, the way he refuses can give you an indication of his mind-set and possible plans. This may in turn suggest the next option you should try.

How to Negotiate

The most effective means of persuasion is the spoken word. Say the right words at the right time and in the right tone of voice, and you can move mountains, turn rivers, or stop an assailant dead in his tracks. To accomplish this, you must:

1. **Be calm and collected.** If your voice communicates fear, anger, or contempt, you will have little chance of reaching your assailant in a positive way. Center yourself, and speak in the calm, easy voice you might use with a good friend or peer. Don't beg or plead. Equality is the best position from which to negotiate, and a pleading tone betrays feelings of inferiority.

2. Empathize with your assailant. To empathize with someone is to feel what he feels, to experience things as he experiences them. Try to identify with your attacker, to sense his wants, needs, and fears. The more commonality you can find, the better you'll be able to speak his language. The more you speak his language, the better you'll be able to persuade him to do what you want. Put yourself in your assailant's shoes for a moment and try to sense what motivates him.

3. Redirect your assailant's plans. Once you've established rapport with your attacker, try to direct his thoughts away from harming you and toward benefiting himself. You will need to assess, through conversation and intuition, what will most effectively engage his self-interest.

When to Negotiate

The most promising times to attempt negotiation are the following:

1. When your assailant has given some sign of being open to approach, that he wants you to like or accept him. Spot these offers of a relationship as early as you can and exploit them. If possible, don't grant acceptance unless your assailant is willing to compromise by, for example, agreeing to unlock the door, put down his weapon, or do something else that is conciliatory.

2. When you and your assailant have an obvious point of similarity such as age, gender, ethnic background, etc. Use this edge of affinity and let your assailant know you understand his problems and concerns.

3. When you need to stall for time. The longer you can keep him talking or listening, the better are your chances. If he won't listen to your appeals, persuade him to talk about his grievances.

4. When your assailant needs your help to back down from a position he's taken, is confused, or is unsure about what to do. Tactfully sum up the situation for him, outlining his options, suggesting that he choose the best alternative for both of you.

When Not to Negotiate

Generally, negotiation may not be your best option in the following circumstances:

1. When there's no time for discussion. Don't waste time searching for words when action is called for. Break off negotiations and do something else.

2. When your assailant isn't capable of understanding you. If he is deaf or doesn't speak your language, trying to communicate may spark frustration and hostility.

3. When your attacker is too deranged or too hostile to respond to reason. In such a case, silence is better than speech. Avoid crying or pleading. Hold your tongue and choose some other option.

---

33 Taking No Action as an Option

Depending on the situation, "no action" ranges from standing stock still in your tracks to continuing whatever you're doing and pretending you haven't noticed anything. If, for example, you walk into a store and a man waving a shotgun shouts "Hold it right there!", the best thing to do is freeze. But if a bunch of young toughs make threatening comments as you walk past, go right on by, pretending you haven't heard them.

It is important to recognize that taking no action can represent a deliberate choice on your part. It is not passive or inadvertent, but a purposeful strategy to achieve to more favorable circumstances. Knowing you have chosen this response gives you confidence and control over yourself, if not over the situation. This control will be helpful later on, when it becomes time to act.

When to Take No Action

Generally, it is appropriate to select "no action" as an option when you're faced with the following kinds of situations or types of people.

1. When you can't do anything anyway. Don't struggle when it won't help. Relax and save your strength for the moment you can really use it.

2. When you can't decide what to do. If you're confused or upset by a sudden situation, wait until your priorities become clear.

3. When the situation is changing for the better. Like a good soup, some situations need time to develop. Just wait; your turn is coming.

4. When you're surrounded, outnumbered, or caught off guard. Roll with the punches, so to speak, and use the centering process to recover your balance and self-control.

5. When your action might jeopardize someone else's life. In a hostage situation or when somebody else will be hurt if you make a move, the best thing you can do is become calm and quiet. Get your priorities in order, and try to think ahead.

6. When someone is going to rob you at gunpoint or knifepoint. Don't move a muscle. The odds are that they want only your money, and money is something you can afford to lose.

7. When you're confronted by someone who is mentally disturbed or under the influence of alcohol and/or drugs. Much depends on your assailant's condition, but the usual advice from drug counselors is to avoid agitating anyone who may already be confused, excited, or erratic. This is especially true of people who have taken Phencyclidine (PCP); their strength is phenomenal and their behavior totally unpredictable.

8. When a captor is holding you or someone else hostage. Unless your life or another person's life is in immediate peril, take no action.

When Taking No Action Is Unwise

Doing nothing is *not* in your best interest in the following circumstances:

1. When there is no advantage in delay. If you recognize that the situation will not improve unless you force the issue, go ahead and take action: fight.

2. When the situation calls for you to run and hide. If you see a chance to escape, do so.

3. When you might be able to talk your way out of the situation. If you see that the assailant might listen to reason, start talking.

4. When doing nothing seems to indicate that you condone the situation. For example, if one person is taunting or victimizing another on the street and a crowd gathers, unless someone makes a statement to the contrary the assailant feels encouraged and protected. If, however, someone speaks out early, it may prevent the assailant from escalating his actions. A good thing to say is "Here come the cops!"

---

34 Surprise or Diversion as an Option

The central objective of this response is to interfere with your assailant's train of thought so that he becomes confused or focuses his attention on something else—thereby giving you a chance either to take control of the situation or to escape. If this change of direction happens suddenly, it's called surprise; if it's the result of a slower process, it's called diversion.

This perhaps apocryphal story, told about Milton Erickson, the renowned clinical hypnotist, illustrates the value of surprise. He turned a corner in New York City late one night to find himself confronted by a robber brandishing a pistol. Waving the gun in Erickson's face, the man demanded: "Know what it is? Know what it is?" Without missing a beat, Erickson looked down at his wristwatch, back at the robber, and calmly replied, "It's exactly quarter past two." The mugger was so taken aback by the unexpectedness of this response that Erickson quickly brushed past him and went on his way.

By staying centered and not letting the robber switch *his* train of thought, Erickson was able to respond in a spontaneous and creative way, stopping his would-be assailant cold.

Here is another example of this kind of tactic. A single mother with a small child was cleaning her apartment one afternoon when a young man, the son of a family friend, arrived at her door. She had had one date with him, which had been mildly unnerving. When he pleaded that he needed to talk to her, she made the mistake of letting him in.

Within minutes it became clear that he was under the influence of some sort of drug. Declaring his love, he began to grab at her while her young child watched. More than anything else, she wanted to protect her child from witnessing a nasty and perhaps traumatic incident, but she sensed that direct rejection or confrontation would be the wrong approach.

Instead, she turned to the young man and, with all the maternal force she could summon, told him that he was hungry and she was going to prepare a hamburger for him. She began bustling around in the kitchen as if nothing unusual were happening and told him to set the table. Her reaction was so different from what he expected that he passively followed orders.

As soon as he began eating, she reminded him that he hadn't seen her sister for years. Then she went to the phone and in a tone of voice that left no room for argument, urged her sister and brother-in-law to come over immediately. The young man became subdued and left shortly after her family arrived.

She still remembers the fear she felt during the entire incident, but she says this fear was outweighed by her determination to protect her child. She chose diversion as an initial strategy because it presented the greatest opportunity for peaceful resolution of the problem.

It isn't really possible to practice surprise or diversion beforehand because it depends on a departure from the expected in any given situation. It is unlikely that a rehearsed response will work in a real situation, and there's nothing worse or more potentially disastrous than a failed surprise. So rather than rehearse specific ploys and tactics, it's more important to be aware of the possibility of changing a situation or of capitalizing on a sudden development that can work to your advantage.

How to Initiate Surprise or Diversion

Generally speaking, the basic ways to surprise or divert your opponent are the following:

1. Make a sudden move. This could be anything from throwing something at your assailant to suddenly going into another room and locking or barricading the door behind you.

2. Say something funny. Taking a humorous view of the situation or cracking a joke when the atmosphere is tense is one of the best ways to get people to let off steam. Especially when things are strained, humor is the last response expected, making it doubly effective.

3. Fall down, fake unconsciousness or a heart attack, vomit, defecate, feign insanity, or freak out. In the right situation, any of these methods can be very disconcerting to an assailant, causing revulsion and alarm. They are not pleasant alternatives, but they have been known to work in certain situations.

4. Scream. A high-pitched scream at close range can be very terrifying, especially if your assailant doesn't expect you to scream (if, for example, you remained silent during the first few moments of the encounter, the attacker expects you to continue to be silent). A good scream will startle your adversary down to his socks, but you must be ready to follow up immediately with some action that will put you in a better position in relation to your opponent.

5. Tell an outright lie. If you're standing on a corner and a frightening character pulls up in a car and asks what you're doing, it's okay to tell him you're waiting for your father, who is the chief of detectives. If a captor asks you if there's a back door to your apartment, tell him there isn't so that later you might be able to use it as a means of escape.

When to Surprise or Divert

The best times to choose this response are in the following circumstances:

1. When your assailant becomes confused, unsure of himself, or uncertain of what his next move should be. This is a good time to take the lead by either directing him to your way of thinking or startling him into making a move that is to your benefit.

2. When there is some kind of external diversion. If a sudden noise, an interruption, or a disagreement with a confederate

takes your assailant's attention away from you, take advantage
of this opportunity to escape, attack, or do something else to
improve your position.

3. When the situation seems hopeless. Try doing or saying the
   weirdest, most unexpected thing you can think of. If things
   can't get any worse, perhaps they'll get better if you try something off the wall.

When Not to Surprise or Divert

Don't attempt surprise or diversion when confronted by the
following kinds of assailants:

1. An attacker who seems professional, calm, and fully alert to his
   surroundings. A professional usually will be conscious of the
   pressure of time. If you try to stall him or divert him, it may
   make the situation worse.

2. An opponent who is excitable, jumpy, and/or has a weapon.
   People on drugs (especially PCP) can be very irritable and para-
   noid, and are likely to fly off the handle at a comparatively
   innocuous occurrence. Do not try to startle these people; serious harm could result.

3. More than one attacker. Unless you're certain that you can
   surprise or divert everybody at the same time, don't choose
   this option. A possible exception to this rule is the use of humor. If you're really funny, everybody may laugh at the same
   time, resulting in a lessening of tension.

---

35 The Blending Option

There's an old tale of a large oak tree standing near a slender
willow. The oak stands tall, proud of its strength and majesty
—until a hurricane strikes. Buffeted by the blasts, the oak re-
sists, rigid and massive, but finds itself no match for the storm.
Some top branches are the first to go, snapped off and sent
flying by the wind and rain. Finally, the tree itself is uprooted

and flung down. When the storm is over and the oak is in splinters, the supple willow still stands. By not resisting the wind, by bending easily with its force, it has ridden out the hurricane. Its very flexibility has assured its survival.

The blending option is the course of the willow. It is also the guiding principle of the art of Aikido. Rather than standing against a stronger, more forceful assailant, you choose instead to move with him, to align and blend your force with his. This involves a fleeting, temporary realignment of your energy so that every ounce of your physical strength and force of will aligns with his. This unexpected addition of force, this sudden surge of extra power surprises, startles, and upsets your adversary. It is more than he bargained for; and puts him off balance for a moment. This instant of confusion and disequilibrium gives you your chance. Since your power is aligned with his, your assertion of a small, almost insignificant amount of force will enable you to take control of him or to run away. Choose either option immediately.

Because blending implies cooperation, alignment, and agreement, it can be used with telling effect during either verbal or physical attacks. The nature of the encounter will tell you on which level to respond.

How to Blend

In applying the principles of blending, you should do the following:

1. Relax completely. Offer no resistance whatsoever but, rather, flow with whatever force is pushing against you. If the attack directed at you can be seen as a stream, then your job is to be the water, not the rock that stands against it.

2. Actively join the force. Turn, twist, wriggle, and spin in the same direction as your attacker's energy. For example, if he is pushing you toward a door, move in that direction at first, and then quickly spin to the side so that you end up behind him. This is the same principle as rolling with the punches in order to be able to control or escape them. The exercises on page 113 and 115 illustrate how this can be done.

3. Empathize with your attacker. Try to feel what he feels, to look at the situation through his eyes. Even if you can't possibly imagine what your adversary's thought process is or why he would attack an innocent, well-meaning person like you, the very act of *trying* to understand puts you that much closer to blending with him. Because the ultimate purpose of blending is to control or evade your attacker, the more you are able to identify with him, the better able you'll be to anticipate his movements and guide them to your own ends. For example, if your assailant tells you he's going to rape you, you might reply (assuming you choose to blend), "Why don't we have a drink first?" or some such accommodating suggestion. If he accepts the blend and you're at home, suggest that he get the ice cubes out of the refrigerator while you get the bourbon. When he turns away, clobber him with the whiskey bottle or slip out of the room and run for help. Sound implausible? It's done all the time.

Blending Exercise No. 1

1. Have a partner stand behind you, placing the palm of one hand in the middle of your back (see illustrations on next page).

2. Ask him to push you slowly and steadily ahead of him as he walks across the room. Rather than resist his force, accommodate it, aligning your speed and direction with his.

3. As soon as both of you are moving in the same direction at the same rate of speed, execute a 360-degree turn. If your movement is a tight, smooth spin, your turn will put you into a close, controlling position behind your still-moving partner, a position from which you can now push *him*.

The key element is spinning tightly and smoothly. If you keep your center of gravity low, relax, and don't resist the force, you will be able to control the force that's trying to control you. If your center of gravity rises—that is, if you try to turn from your head or shoulders rather than from your center—your spin will be unstable, leaving you off balance and out of control. Turn from your center point, letting it lead you through the spin.

Blending Exercise No. 2

1. Face your partner and have him put his hand in the center of

Blending Exercise No. 1.

your chest, pushing you backward ahead of him. Don't resist the force, but blend with it.

2. Once you and he are moving synchronously, execute a 180-degree turn from your center point. This will allow you to arrive at a position slightly to the side of your partner, facing in the same direction.

It is more difficult to turn while moving backward than forward, but keeping your center is still the essential point to remember while you're turning.

Blending Exercise No. 3
In this exercise, you blend with someone who is pulling you in a direction you don't want to go. This enables you to release yourself.

1. Stand facing your partner and have him grab your left wrist with his right hand, pulling you slowly and steadily across the room. Initially, resist his force, and ask him to pull harder.

2. As soon as he does so, withdraw your opposition and surge toward him. Unable to handle this unexpected accommodation, your partner will stumble backward.

3. As he does so, suddenly reverse your direction again and move sharply in the opposite direction.

When to Blend

The most opportune situations in which to choose the blending response are the following:

1. When you have no other choice. If the attacker is either so swift or so remorseless that you have no time to recover from the initial onslaught, blend with the force in progress.

2. When you need time to decide which of the other options best suits your situation. Blending is a good and active alternative to taking no action when you need time to think or when you must wait until the time is proper for you to act.

Chapter Seven

Securing Professional Assistance

Nowadays, if you are a victim of crime, more help is available than ever before. Special programs offering financial assistance and psychological counseling have been initiated during the past few years. The police are your first link to these programs—in fact, some are run under police auspices. We recommend taking advantage of these services, because the more support you have after a violent incident the more easily you will be able to put your life back together.

36 Financial Help for the Victims of Crime

California was the first state in the country to institute a program specializing in monetary compensation for victims of violent crimes. A 1981 amendment to the California Penal Code specifies that people who have suffered psychological injury are also eligible for financial compensation from the state. A member of the government agency handling these claims says that psychological victimization is usually the result of a family member or close friend witnessing the killing or maiming of a loved one during a violent crime. For example, a mother who witnessed her son's death in a hit-and-run accident would be eligible for compensation. California will honor up to $10,000 in medical expenses and $10,000 for loss of wages.

At least thirty other states have followed California's lead in setting up similar compensation programs. The policies governing the amount of money received for claims differ from state to state. Contact the local office of your state representative or the board of control in your state capital to determine if a similar program exists and to ascertain its eligibility requirements.

---

37 Assistance for Rape Victims

By definition, forcing a person to engage in sexual intercourse against her will or his will constitutes the criminal act of rape. A study in a large Boston hospital identified three separate categories of this crime:

1. *Rape trauma*—forced violent sexual contact without consent.

2. *Inability to consent*—typically, an attack on a child by an adult who stands in some position of authority.

3. *Sex-stress rape*—initial consent with ensuing violence.

In this study, as is generally true of reported rapes, the vast majority were in the first category of rape trauma. However, the others are worthy of mention since all rape victims are in need of assistance and support.

If you are a victim of rape, do the following:

1. Seek medical attention as soon after the incident as possible. Law-enforcement authorities recommend the following procedure, because it preserves physical evidence essential to prosecuting rape:

   a. Report the crime to the police.

b. Do not wash, bathe, shower, or douche.

c. Have a medical examination as soon as possible. The police will arrange for this.

d. Make sure the doctor records any internal or external injuries and takes semen smears.

e. Show police, and also a friend or relative, any external injuries or bruises.

f. Give police any torn or stained clothes or undergarments.

g. Make sure a test is done for VD and that a followup test is taken two weeks later.

2. Seek medical attention immediately, even if you are unwilling to report the crime. We believe that rape incidents should be reported but understand that in certain unusual situations you may not wish to do so. Even in these circumstances, though, medical help is necessary—and available. Private physicians will keep your confidentiality, as will doctors and nurses in hospital emergency rooms if you demand that they do so. Their records can be subpoenaed by the courts, however, so the surest protection is simply to say that you are seeking attention for "painful and unprotected intercourse."

3. Seek counseling at your nearest rape-treatment center. One of the significant achievements of the women's movement is the establishment of rape-treatment centers and hotlines in nearly every major community in the country. Local authorities can tell you how to contact your nearest center, or you can write to Rape Crisis Center, P.O. Box 21005, Washington, D.C. 20009. This organization advises victims about all sexual crimes including rape.

　　These centers provide individual and group counseling, usually on a short-term basis. Persons who have been through these programs generally give them very high marks, stating that the emotional support they received made all the difference in getting through a very difficult and traumatic time. Experts in the field recommend that you seek assistance as soon after the incident as possible, but they add that even if you were a victim of rape in the past, it's never too late to reach out for help.

38 Help for Victims of Other Crimes

Professionals in the mental-health field agree that victims of violent crime need special support in the period after the incident. How people react is very much based on the severity of their situation, their personalities, and their prior experience. Some become very depressed, or anxious, or even physically ill; others seem to take the incident in stride but suffer after-effects later. Still others, with a history of handling stress well, bounce back easily if their personal support systems are there.

Community mental-health centers and district attorneys' offices are beginning to recognize the need for special services and are establishing them. Even if there is no special program in your area, trained professionals offer counseling through these mental-health centers, usually on a sliding-scale fee basis or at no cost at all. Check with your local mental-health association or the National Council of Community Mental Health Centers, Washington, D.C., for the location closest to you.

Chapter Eight

Providing Assistance

Every day all over this country there are people who go out of their way to help strangers in trouble. If you've ever been on the receiving end of this kind of assistance, you know the special feeling of gratitude you feel toward your deliverer. If you've ever been on the giving end, you know these special rewards as well.

Nonetheless, helping another person can cause you trouble. Interfering where you have no business or where you're not wanted is a sure way to attract hostility; acting inappropriately can be downright dangerous. It is therefore important to know how and when to provide assistance.

In this chapter we will discuss some ways of dealing with these complexities and provide suggestions concerning how everyone can help.

39 Reporting the Incident

It is important to report any crime you witness. Even if all you do is report the incident to the police or tell neighbors exactly what happened, you will have taken some of the burden from the victim, and possibly you will have done something to spare a future victim.

Even if others have already spoken to the authorities, something you saw might be of great assistance in determining what happened and who was responsible. You may also find that telling your story to police has psychological benefits, because witnessing a crime is usually distressing in that it leaves the victim feeling powerless. There is also something very satisfying in behaving like a good citizen. If you feel that becoming involved places you in personal jeopardy, secure a promise of police protection.

When you report a crime to the police—either by phone or in person—prepare yourself before you speak. Review the events and get them in proper order. Give as much detail as possible. Center yourself, become as composed as possible, and speak slowly and distinctly. Don't get upset if you are asked for personal details, such as your name and address, before giving your account. Simply concentrate on telling your side of things as simply and completely as you can.

40 Observing and Describing Assailants

If you see the assailants, observe them as closely as you can so that you can provide descriptions. But do so with caution, as they could become enraged or vindictive. Conceal your interest, but note sex, approximate age, race, height, weight, and color of hair, eyes, etc. Try to recall any peculiarities of dress, speech, walk, or gait, or any unusual physical characteristics, such as scars or tattoos. If you see weapons, take similar note of them. If possible, write down the make, model, and license number of car. Pay special attention to anything that is touched so that the police can lift fingerprints.

41 Becoming a "Safe and Alive" Good Samaritan

A recent news report told of a doctor who had sprinted across four lanes of freeway traffic to pull a man from a burning car.

When asked what had gone through his mind, the doctor answered that his only concern had been to preserve the victim's life. In this, as in many other cases of Samaritan-like benevolence, the person felt compelled to act even though this meant exposing himself to considerable danger or death.

These acts of heroism are obviously spontaneous and exceptional, even though their occurrence is more frequent than is generally acknowledged. However, it is more typical to experience confusion of fear when you witness a life-threatening situation. Should you intercede? If so, what is the best way to do so without exposing yourself to unnecessary risk? What if you don't feel like getting involved at all? While there are no easy answers to these questions, we believe that the fabric of society is held together in part by people reaching out to assist one another, especially in times of trouble. On the other hand, we also feel that you have the right to protect your own safety in so doing.

The following examples, guidelines, and options will, we hope, be of some assistance, although ultimately your intuition and personal sense of right and wrong will dictate your response.

1. Report any crime or suspicious incident to the authorities as soon as possible.

2. Call the authorities if you see a motorist in trouble. Write down the color and make of the car, its license number, and its location to ease identification. (See Section 5 in Chapter One— "Security in Your Car"—for the safest way to approach motorists in distress.)

3. If necessary, render first aid or CPR (cardiopulmonary resuscitation) until professional help arrives. The appendix of this book describes basic first-aid instructions that can save a victim's life. We highly recommend the CPR course, offered either free of charge or at a very low fee by many community organizations.

4. Take a moment and get centered if you see someone under attack. How many assailants are there? What is the nature of the attack? Do they have any weapons?

5. Then consider the following options, always keeping in mind never to use more force than is absolutely necessary.

   a. Fighting off the attackers.

   b. Fleeing and immediately summoning the authorities.

   c. Bargaining with the attackers. Perhaps you can persuade them that it is in their best interests not to commit the crime. Perhaps you can order them to stop. Or perhaps you can pretend that you've already called the authorities, if this would be convincing.

   d. Using a shriek alarm or police whistle.

   e. Screaming in the most piercing tones possible.

   f. Convincing other bystanders to assist you in thwarting the attack.

   g. Pretending to join the attack. This is similar to the blending option described in Chapter Six. If one person is hitting another, you might be able to approach the assailant by cheering or egging him on, which might allow you to get close enough to fight him off.

   h. Doing nothing for the moment. If, for example, you were on a bus or subway that was invaded by a horde of teenage gang members, you probably couldn't prevent them from striking another passenger. In that case, it would be best to sit tight, staring at the floor. When the incident is over, give aid to the victim.

   i. Creating a diversion of some sort. (See the story in Epilogue for an unusual example.)

6. Become a good Samaritan before a crime occurs. Help friends, acquaintances, and the elderly in your community to burglar-proof their homes if you have the skills and resources and they do not.

   Not everyone can risk his or her life to save another, but that doesn't mean there is nothing you can do. Helping in any of the ways described in this section or in other ways that we may not have mentioned, or simply sharing what you know about crime prevention, creates a more positive social environment and support for those in need of your help. With this comes that very special feeling that accompanies giving of yourself.

Chapter Nine

Protecting Your Children

Children face many of the same dangers as adults, although there are certain crimes that can be described as child-directed, such as sexual molestation. The central challenge that parents face is to instill in their children a sense of caution without making the children unnecessarily fearful.

To accomplish this, plan what you want to tell a child. His or her age, the crime situation in your neighborhood, and what the child already knows will influence the nature of this discussion. How your child will respond is similarly determined by his or her nature, your tone of voice, and the clarity with which you set down safety guidelines. Children beyond the age of five or six may already have good ideas concerning safety rules and should be encouraged to participate in drawing up family safety precautions.

42 What Children Should Be Told

These are the main points to emphasize with your child.

1. You should know your full name, address, phone number, school, and the name and phone number of a relative or friend who can be contacted in case of emergency.

2. Never tell a stranger that you are home alone. Tell a caller at the door or on the phone that your mother, father, or whoever is taking care of you is taking a nap and can't talk right now.

3. Always discuss with a parent any incident that has confused or disturbed you, no matter how minor. If anyone approaches you in a frightening manner, tell your parents, a teacher, or a policeman.

4. If you walk to school, go with another child from the neighborhood rather than alone.

5. Don't play or walk in alleys, vacant lots, or deserted areas.

6. Keep away from strangers. If they offer you candy, money, or anything else, walk away as if they don't exist. If they tell you that your parents sent them, don't believe them.

7. If you need to use a public restroom, take a friend along if possible. If there are problems in the restrooms in your school, tell your teacher and get your teacher's permission to take a classmate with you. Also, tell your parents so they can help the school set up a safety program.

8. If you have a bicycle, get a good lock and be sure to use it.

9. Don't fight someone who is bigger and stronger than you, or who has a weapon, if he tries to steal your money or other valuables. Your physical safety is more important than anything you own. Tell your family immediately, or tell school authorities if it happens on the schoolground.

10. If someone harms you in any way and then makes you promise you won't tell, you don't have to keep this promise. Tell your parents, a teacher, or the police.

11. If you see a crime taking place, get away from the scene as quickly as possible and let your parents or the police know. Don't try to help unless the criminals are no longer in sight.

12. If you're lost or need help, try to find a police officer or a phone. Always carry one or two "safety" dimes so you can make a

phone call. If you don't have money and you can't find a police officer, approach a woman rather than a man for assistance.

---

43 Child Molestation

Explain the dangers of sexual molestation to your children in simple, easy-to-understand language. Unless children are very young, they may be more aware of this problem than you might assume. Prime-time television shows, even in the eight-to-nine P.M. "family hour," have been devoted to this topic.

First and foremost, tell your children that no one has the right to invade the privacy of their bodies or to fondle them. Make sure they understand the difference between this and normal affection from relatives and friends.

Since children are sometimes attacked by people they know, be very careful about those to whom you entrust your child's care. If a child tells you he or she has been molested, take the child seriously, no matter how painful the revelation. Even if you doubt the child, seek professional counseling. Your local social-work department or community mental-health center can help.

In circumstances where it is clear that the child has been molested, take the following actions:

1. Seek medical attention.

2. Make sure the child understands that he or she did nothing wrong. It is not unusual for children to feel guilty.

3. Control your emotional responses in front of the child in order to avoid frightening him or her even more; express your anger or other emotions only with other adults. If you can't control your anger, make sure your child understands that it is directed toward the molester.

4. Seek short-term professional counseling if your child or other family members have problems in dealing with the molestation.

5. When everyone's emotions have calmed down, sit down with the child to discuss how such situations might be avoided in the future.

Fortunately, children are resiliant, especially if situations like this are handled wisely and calmly. In fact, wisdom is the key in this entire area. Children need a balanced view—an understanding that most adults and other children have no desire to hurt them, that their parents can protect them from most sources of harm, and, finally, that they can protect themselves by following the guidelines you have established.

Epilogue

A Soft Answer

The main thrust of this book has been hard advice. It is primarily a primer of well-known commonsense ways of protecting yourself and your family. Ms.Shepherd-Chow and I agree with authorities that you should follow these guidelines.

However, our account would be incomplete if it did not discuss those situations where a soft answer best turns away wrath, which is an approach to conflict resolution that is best illustrated by a personal story.

A turning point in my life came one day on a train in the suburbs of Tokyo in the middle of a drowsy spring afternoon. The old car clanking and rattling over the rails was comparatively empty—a few housewives with their kids in tow, some old folks out shopping, a couple of off-duty bartenders studying the racing form. I gazed absently at the drab houses and dusty hedgerows.

At one station the doors opened and suddenly the quiet afternoon was shattered by a man bellowing at the top of his lungs, yelling violent, obscene, incomprehensible curses. Just as the doors closed, the man, still yelling, staggered into our car. He was big, drunk, and dirty, dressed in laborer's clothing. His bulging eyes were demonic, neon red. His hair was crusted with filth. Screaming, he swung at the first person he saw, a woman holding a baby. The blow glanced off her shoulder, sending her spinning into the laps of an elderly couple. It was a miracle that the baby was unharmed.

The terrified couple jumped up and scrambled toward the other end of the car. The laborer aimed a kick at the retreating back of the old lady, but he missed and she scuttled to safety. This so enraged the drunk that he grabbed the metal pole in the center of the car and tried to wrench it out of its stanchion. I could see that one of his hands was cut and bleeding. The train lurched ahead, the passengers frozen with fear.

I stood up. At the time, I was young, in pretty good shape, was six feet tall, and weighed 225 pounds. I'd been putting in a solid eight hours of Aikido training every day for the past three years and thought I was tough. The trouble was, my martial skill was untested in actual combat. As a student of Aikido, I was not allowed to fight.

My teacher, the founder of Aikido, taught us each morning that the art was devoted to peace. "Aikido," he said again and again, "is the art of reconciliation. Whoever has the mind to fight has broken his connection with the universe. If you try to dominate other people, you are already defeated. We study how to resolve conflict, not how to start it."

I listened to his words. I tried hard. I wanted to quit fighting. I had even gone so far as to cross the street a few times to avoid the *chimpira*, the pinball punks who lounged around the train stations. They'd have been happy to test my martial ability. My forbearance exalted me. I felt both tough and holy. In my heart of hearts, however, I was dying to be a hero. I wanted a chance, an absolutely legitimate opportunity whereby I might save the innocent by destroying the guilty.

"This is it!" I said to myself as I got to my feet. "This slob, this animal, is drunk and mean and violent. People are in danger. If I don't do something fast, someone will probably get hurt."

Seeing me stand up, the drunk saw a chance to focus his rage. "Aha!" he roared. "A foreigner! You need a lesson in Japanese manners!" He punches the metal pole once to give weight to his words.

Hanging on lightly to the commuter strap overhead, I gave him a slow look of disgust and dismissal—every bit of nastiness I could summon up. I planned to take this turkey apart, but he had to be the one to move first. And I wanted him mad, because the madder he got, the more certain my victory. I pursed my lips and blew him a sneering, insolent kiss that hit him like a slap in the face. "All right!" he hollered. "You're gonna get a lesson." He gathered himself for a rush at me. He would never know what hit him.

A split second before he moved, someone shouted "Hey!" It was ear-splitting. I remember being struck by the strangely joyous, lilting quality of it, as though you and a friend had been searching diligently for something and had suddenly stumbled upon it. "Hey!"

I wheeled to my left, the drunk spun to his right. We both stared down at a little old Japanese. He must have been well into his seventies. He took no notice of me but beamed delightedly at the laborer, as though he had a most important, most welcome secret to share.

"C'mere," the old man said in an easy vernacular, beckoning to the drunk. "C'mere and talk with me." He waved his hand lightly. The big man followed, as if on a string. He planted his feet belligerently in front of the old gentleman, towering threateningly over him. "Talk to you," he roared above the clanking wheels. "Why the hell should I talk to you?"

The old man continued to beam at the laborer. There was not a trace of fear or resentment about him. "What'cha been drinking?" he asked lightly, his eyes sparkling with interest.

"I been drinkin' sake," the laborer bellowed back, "and it's none of your goddam business!" Flecks of spittle spattered the old man.

"Oh, that's wonderful," the old man said with delight. "Absolutely wonderful! You see, I love sake, too. Every night, me and my wife (she's seventy-six, you know), we warm up a little bottle of sake and take it out into the garden, and we sit on the old wooden bench that my grandfather's first student made for him. We watch the sun go down, and we look to see how our persimmon tree is doing. My great-grandfather planted that tree, you know, and we worry about whether it will recover from those ice storms we had last winter. Persimmons do not do well after ice storms, although I must say that ours has done rather better than I expected, especially when you consider the poor quality of the soil. Still, it is most gratifying to watch when we take our sake and go out to enjoy the evening—even when it rains!" He looked up at the laborer, eyes twinkling, happy to share his delightful information.

As he struggled to follow the intricacies of the old man's conversation, the drunk's face began to soften. His fists slowly unclenched. "Yeah," he said slowly, "I love persimmons, too..." His voice trailed off.

"Yes," said the old man, smiling, "and I'm sure you have a wonderful wife."

"No," replied the laborer. "My wife died." He hung his head. Very gently, swaying with the motion of the train, the big man began to sob. "I don't got no wife. I don't got no home. I don't got no job. I don't got no money. I don't got nowhere to go." Tears rolled down his cheeks, and a spasm of pure despair rippled through his body. Above the baggage rack a four-color ad trumpeted the virtues of suburban luxury living.

Now it was my turn. Standing there in my well-scrubbed youthful innocence, my make-this-world-safe-for-democracy righteousness, I suddenly felt dirtier than the drunk was.

Just then the train arrived at my stop. The platform was packed, and the crowd surged into the car as soon as the doors opened. Maneuvering my way out, I heard the old man cluck sympathetically. "My, my," he said with undiminished delight. "That is a very difficult predicament, indeed. Sit down here and tell me about it."

I turned my head for one last look. The laborer was sprawled like a sack on the seat, his head in the old man's lap. The old man looked down at him, all compassion and delight, one hand softly stroking the filthy, matted head.

As the train pulled away, I sat down on a bench. What I had wanted to do with muscle and meanness had been accomplished with a few kind words. I had seen Aikido tried in combat, and the essence of it was love, as the founder had said. I would have to practice the art with an entirely different spirit. It would be a long time before I could speak about the resolution of conflict.

We can't recommend the old man's way of dealing with potential violence as a simple strategy, like locking your doors or putting your valuables in a hotel safe. His insight, compassion, and fearlessness are qualities to be emulated, not mimicked. But we ask you to keep them in mind because within each of us is such a capacity for wisdom.

Because of the old man, all of us on the train were able to leave safe and alive. We offer this book in the hope it will be of similar service.

Appendix

Survival Guide: What to Do in an Emergency Until Medical Help Is Available

We would like to thank the Pacific Telephone Company for permission to reprint its excellent Survival Guide. In it you will find instructions concerning emergency first aid. We include it because lives can be saved in those precious minutes before professional assistance arrives.

In a major disaster, phone lines to emergency medical services may be overloaded or damaged. These pages will help you know what to do until medical help is available.

A sudden illness or physical injury can strike *anyone* at *any time.* More that 100,000 Americans die from accidents each year. Ten million suffer disabling injuries. Medical authorities state that an alarming number of these people die or are disabled needlessly for lack of proper care immediately after the accident or at the start of the illness. They suggest that you carefully read the following pages and also take a first-aid course from the American Red Cross.

When a person stops *breathing,* death may occur in *four to six minutes.*

When a person is *bleeding* badly, unless the bleeding is stopped, about *fifteen minutes* of life may remain.

Remember: In an emergency, seconds and minutes can make the difference between *life and death.* Decisive, quick, and proper *action by you* can save a life!

The Call for Help

1. If an injured person is in distress but is breathing, phone for help at once.

2. If the victim is not breathing, help first and phone later—or get someone else to phone.

3. What to say:

   a. Give the phone number from which you are calling.

   b. Give the address and any special instructions on how to get to the victim.

   c. Describe the victim's condition as best you can—burned, bleeding, broken bones, etc.

   d. Give your name.

   e. Do not hang up! Let emergency persons end the conversation. They may have questions to ask you or special information to give you about what you can do until help arrives.

Breathing

Choking

Anything stuck in the throat blocking the air passage can stop breathing and cause unconsciousness and death within four to six minutes.

1. Do not interfere with a choking victim who can speak, cough, or breathe. However, if the choking continues without lessening, call for emergency medical help.

2. If the victim cannot speak, cough, or breathe, immediately have someone call for emergency medical help while you take the following action.

   a. For a conscious victim

      (1) Stand just behind and to the side of the victim, who can be standing or sitting. Support the victim with one hand on the chest. The victim's head should be lowered. Give four sharp blows between the shoulder blades. If unsuccessful, go to step **2**.

      (2) Stand behind the victim, who can be standing or sitting. Wrap your arms around his/her middle just above the navel. Clasp your hands together in a doubled fist and press in and up in quick thrusts. Repeat several times. If still unsuccessful, repeat four back blows and four quick thrusts until the victim is no longer choking or becomes unconscious.

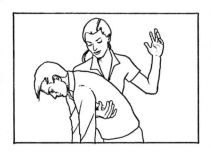 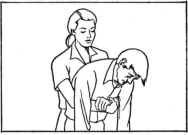

   b. For an unconscious victim

      (1) Place the victim on the floor or ground and give rescue breathing. (See Rescue Breathing section.) If the victim does not start breathing and it appears that your air is not going into the victim's lungs, go to step **2**.

(2) Roll the victim onto his/her side, facing you, with the victim's chest against your knee and give four sharp blows between the shoulder blades. If the victim still does not start breathing, go to step 3.

(3) Roll the victim onto his/her back and give one or more manual thrusts. To give the thrusts, place one of your hands on top of the other with the heel of the bottom hand in the middle of the abdomen, slightly above the navel and below the rib cage. Press into the victim's abdomen with a quick upward thrust. Do not press to either side. Repeat four times if needed. Even if successful, go to step 4.

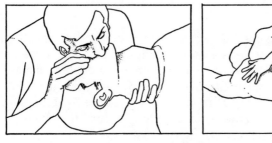
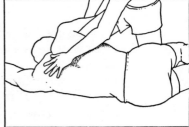
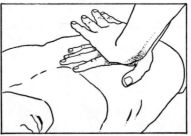

(4) Clear the airway.

a. Hold the victim's mouth open with one hand, using your thumb to depress the tongue.

b. Make a hook with the pointer finger of your other hand and, in a gentle sweeping motion, reach into the victim's throat and feel for a swallowed foreign object which may be blocking the air passage. Repeat the following until successful: **(1)** four back blows; **(2)** four abdominal thrusts; **(3)** probe in mouth; **(4)** try to inflate lungs.

Repeat process.

 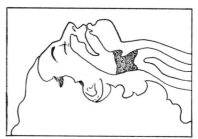

3. If the object has not been retrieved but the swallower suddenly seems all right, play it safe—take him/her directly to the hospital. This is especially critical if the swallowed object is a fish bone, chicken bone, or other jagged object that could do internal damage as it passes through the victim's system.

Unconscious Person

Breathing is the most critical thing we must do to stay alive. A primary cause of death is lack of air.

Be careful approaching an unconscious person. He/she may be in contact with electrical current. If that is the case, turn off the electricity before you touch the victim.

There are hundreds of other possible causes of unconsciousness, but the first thing you must check for is breathing.

1. Try to awaken the victim. Shake his/her shoulders vigorously and shout: "Are you all right?"

2. If there is no response, check for signs of breathing.

a. Be sure the victim is lying flat on his/her back. If you have to roll the victim over, move his/her entire body at one time.

b. Loosen tight clothing around the neck and chest.

3. Open the airway.

    a. If there are no signs of head or neck injuries, tilt the neck gently with one hand.

    b. Push down and back on the forehead with the other hand as you tip the head back.

    c. Place your ear close to the victim's mouth. Listen for breath sounds. Watch his/her chest and stomach for movement. Check for at least five seconds.

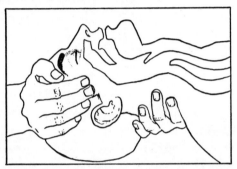

    d. If there is any question in your mind, or if breathing is so faint that you are unsure, assume the worst.

    e. Give rescue breathing immediately. (See Rescue Breathing section.) Have someone else summon professional help.

Rescue Breathing

It may take several hours to revive someone. Keep up rescue breathing until help arrives to relieve you. Remember that you are doing the breathing for the victim. If you stop, in about four to six minutes he/she could be dead. Even if the victim begins to breathe on his/her own, call for professional help.

1. Giving mouth-to-mouth rescue breathing to adults.

    a. Put your hand on the victim's forehead, pinching the nose shut with your fingers, while holding the forehead back.

    b. Your other hand is under the victim's neck supporting and lifting up slightly to maintain an open airway.

c. Take a deep breath. Open your mouth wide and place it over the victim's mouth. Blow air into the victim until you see his/her chest rise.

d. Remove your mouth from the victim's. Turn your head to the side and watch the chest for a falling movement while you listen for air escaping from the victim's mouth as he/she exhales.

e. If you hear air escaping and see the chest fall, you know that rescue breathing is working. Continue until help arrives.

f. Repeat the cycle every five seconds. Twelve breaths per minute.

2. Giving mouth-to-mouth rescue breathing to infants and small children.

a. Be careful tilting a small child's head back to clear the airway. It should *not* be tilted as far back as an adult's. If tilted back too far, it will make the obstruction worse.

b. Cover the child's mouth and nose with your mouth.

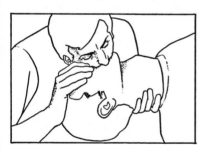
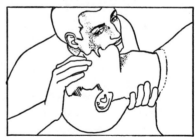
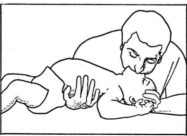

    c. Blow air in with less pressure than for an adult. Give small puffs. A child needs less.

    d. Feel the chest inflate as you blow.

    e. Listen for exhales.

    f. Repeat once every three seconds. Twenty breaths per minute.

Drowning

Drowning is a major cause of accidental death in the United States. Victims of drowning can die within about four to six minutes of the accident because they have stopped breathing.

1. Get the victim out of the water at once.

    a. Use extreme caution to avoid direct contact with the victim, since a panicked victim may drown the rescuer as well.

    b. If the victim is conscious, push a floating object to him/her or let the victim grasp a long branch, pole, or object.

    c. If the victim is unconscious, take a flotation device with you, if possible, and approach him/her with caution. Once ashore or on the deck of a pool, the victim should be placed on his/her back.

2. If the victim is not breathing, start mouth-to-mouth rescue breathing immediately. (See Rescue Breathing section.) Keep giving rescue breathing until the victim can breathe unassisted. That can take an hour or two. Pace yourself. Keep calm. Remember: Even when the victim is breathing unassisted he/she may be in need of medical attention. Have someone else go

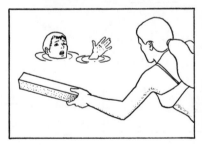

for help. Do not leave the victim alone under any circumstances, not even to call for help.

3. If the victim is breathing without assistance, even though coughing and sputtering, he/she will get rid of the remaining water. You need only stand by to see that recovery continues, but have someone else send for professional help immediately.

Electric Shock (Electrocution)

Normal electrical current can be deadly, and it is all around us.

1. Do not touch a person who has been in contact with electrical current until you are certain that the electricity has been turned off. Shut off the power at the plug, circuit breaker, or fuse box.

2. If the victim is in contact with a wire or a downed power line, use a dry stick to move it away.

3. Check for breathing. If the victim's breathing is weak or has stopped, give rescue breathing immediately. (See Rescue Breathing section.)

4. Call for emergency help. While you wait for help to arrive:

   a. Keep the victim warm (covered with a blanket, coat, jacket, etc.).

   b. Give the victim nothing to drink or eat until he/she has been seen by a doctor.

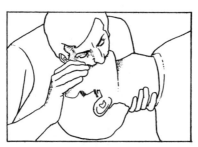

Heart Attack

Heart attack is the number-one killer of adults over the age of thirty-eight. Many heart-attack victims die needlessly because they do not get help in time.

1. Warning signs include:

    a. Severe squeezing pains in the chest.

    b. Pain that radiates from the chest into either the arm, the neck, or the jaw.

    c. Sweating and weakness, nausea or vomiting.

    d. Pain that extends across the shoulders to the back.

2. If the victim is experiencing any of these sensations, take no chances. Call for emergency help at once.

3. Two critical life-threatening things happen to the victim of a heart attack:

    a. Breathing slows down or stops.

    b. The heart slows down or stops pumping blood.

4. If the victim is not breathing, give rescue breathing immediately. (See Rescue Breathing section.) Have someone else call for emergency help.

5. Try to detect a heartbeat by taking a pulse at the carotid artery, which can be felt on either side of the neck slightly below and forward of the base of the jaw.

6. If you cannot detect a heartbeat, CPR (cardiopulmonary resuscitation) should be given to the victim, along with rescue breathing. However, CPR should be given only by a person who is properly trained and certified.

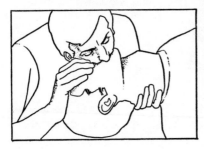 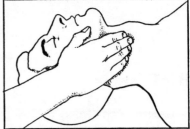

7. Learn CPR. CPR is a way of forcing the heart to continue pumping blood (carrying oxygen) through the lungs and out to the rest of the body where it is needed if life is to continue. CPR is too complicated to be taught from printed pages alone. Four-hour courses are offered by the American Heart Association and the American Red Cross. Many medical authorities agree that everyone thirteen years of age and older should learn both CPR and rescue breathing.

Bleeding

Controlling Bleeding

The best way to control bleeding is with direct pressure over the site of the wound.

1. Use a pad of sterile gauze, if one is available. A sanitary napkin, a clean handkerchief, or even your bare hand, if necessary, will do.

2. Apply firm, steady direct pressure for five to fifteen minutes. Most bleeding will stop within a few minutes.

3. If bleeding is from a foot, hand, leg, or arm, use gravity to help slow the flow of blood. Elevate the limb so that it is higher off the ground than the victim's heart.

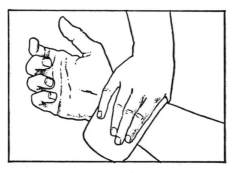

Head Injuries

1. Special care must be taken when trying to stop any scalp bleeding when there is a suspected skull fracture. (If there is bleed-

ing from an ear it usually means that there is a skull fracture.) Bleeding from the scalp can be very heavy even when the injury is not too serious.

2. Don't press too hard. Be extremely careful when applying pressure over the wound so that bone chips from a possible fracture will not be pressed into the brain.

3. Always suspect a neck injury when there is a serious head injury. Immobilize the head and neck.

4. Call for emergency help. Let a professional medical person clean the wound and stitch it, if necessary.,

5. Do not give alcohol or other drugs. They may mask important symptoms.

Internal Bleeding

Warning signs: coughing or vomiting up blood or "coffee ground" material; passing blood in urine or stool; passing black tarlike bowel movements. All require immediate medical attention.

1. Have the victim lie flat and breathe deeply.

2. Do not let the victim take any medication or fluids by mouth until seen by a doctor who permits it.

3. Obtain emergency medical help immediately.

Broken Bones

Broken bones usually do not kill. Do not move the victim, unless he/she is in *immediate danger* of further injury.

1. Check for:

   a. Breathing. Give rescue breathing if needed. (See Rescue Breathing section.)

   b. Bleeding. Apply direct pressure over the site.

   c. Shock. Keep the victim calm and warm.

2. Call for emergency help.

3. Do not try to push the broken bone back into place if it is sticking out of the skin. Do apply a moist dressing to prevent drying out.

4. Do not try to straighten out a fracture. Let a doctor or a trained person do that.

5. Do not permit the victim to walk about.

6. Splint unstable fractures to prevent painful motion.

Seizure

It is an alarming sight—a person whose limbs jerk violently, whose eyes may roll upward, whose breath may become heavy with dribbling or even frothing at the mouth. Breathing may stop in some seizures, or the victim may bite his/her tongue so severely that it blocks the airway. Do not attempt to force anything into the victim's mouth. You may injure the victim and yourself.

1. During the seizure

    a. There is little you can do to stop the seizure.

    b. Call for help.

    c. Let the seizure run its course.

    d. Help the victim to lie down and keep him/her from falling, to avoid injury.

    e. Loosen restrictive clothing.

    f. Use no force.

    g. Do not try to restrain a seizure victim.

2. After the seizure

    a. Check to see if the victim is breathing. If he/she is not, give rescue breathing at once. (See Rescue Breathing section.)

    b. Check to see if the victim is wearing a Medic Alert or similar bracelet. It describes emergency medical requirements.

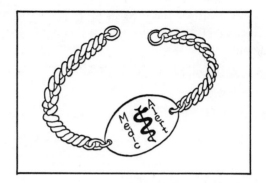

c. Check to see if the victim has any burns around the mouth. This would indicate poison.

3. The victim of a seizure or convulsion may be conscious but confused and not talkative when the intense movement stops. Stay with the victim. Be certain that breathing continues. Then, when the victim seems able to move, get medical attention.

Poisoning

The home is loaded with poisons: cosmetics, detergents, bleaches, cleaning solutions, glue, lye, paint, turpentine, kerosene, gasoline and other petroleum products, alcohol, aspirin and other medications, and on and on.

1. Small children are most often the victims of accidental poisoning. If a child has swallowed or is suspected to have swallowed any substance that might be poisonous, assume the worst— *take action.*

2. Call your Poison Control Center. If none is in your area, call your emergency medical rescue squad. Bring the suspected item and its container with you.

3. If the victim is unconscious, make sure he/she is breathing. If not, tilt the head back and perform mouth-to-mouth breathing. Do not give anything by mouth. Do not attempt to stimulate the victim. Call emergency rescue squad immediately.

4. If the victim is vomiting, roll him/her over onto the left side so that the person will not choke on what is brought up.

5. Be prepared. Determine and verify your Poison Control Center and Fire Department rescue squad numbers and keep them near your telephone.

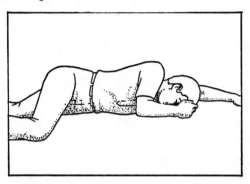

Drug Overdose

A drug overdose is a poisoning. Alcohol is as much a poison as stimulants, tranquilizers, narcotics, hallucinogens, or inhalants. Don't take drunkenness lightly. Too much alcohol can kill, and alcohol in combination with certain other drugs can also be deadly.

1. Call for emergency help at once.

2. Check the victim's breathing and pulse. If breathing has stopped or is very weak, give rescue breathing. (See Rescue Breathing section.) Caution: Victims being revived of alcohol poisoning can be violent. Be careful! They can harm themselves and others.

3. While waiting for help:

   a. Watch breathing.

   b. Cover the victim with a blanket for warmth.

   c. Do not throw water on the victim's face.

   d. Do not give liquor or a stimulant.

Burns

1. Minor burns caused by fire, covering only a small area of the body

    a. Treat with cold running water for twenty to thirty minutes to relieve swelling and pain.

    b. Do not use grease of any kind. Grease traps heat and continues the burning process.

2. Serious burns

    a. These require prompt professional care. Call for help immediately.

    b. Wrap the victim in a clean, wet sheet or towel moistened at room temperature.

    c. Do not attempt to clean the burns or remove clothing or other particles attached to the burned area.

    d. Keep the victim lying down, calm, and reassured.

3. Eye burns

Flush with large amounts of water. Then cover the eye with a damp, clean towel and get emergency medical care as soon as possible.

4. Electrical burns

    a. These are difficult to detect. A person who has received a severe electrical shock may be badly burned internally, though the surface skin shows little evidence.

    b. Get the victim prompt medical attention. Unattended electrical burns can lead to serious complications.

5. Chemical burns

    a. Wash with plenty of cool running water. Get the victim into a cool shower, if possible.

    b. Remove all chemical-soaked clothing immediately, avoiding contact with the soiled part.

    c. After ten minutes, wrap victim in a clean, wet sheet and get emergency medical attention without delay.

6. Smoke Inhalation

    a. If trapped in smoke-filled room or space, stay low; crawl, if necessary, to nearest exit.

    b. Cover nose and mouth with damp cloth if possible.

Recommended Reading

Against Our Will by Susan Brownmiller. (New York: Simon & Schuster, 1975.)

Against Rape by Andra Medea and Kathleen Thompson. (New York: Farrar, Straus & Giroux, 1974.)

Aikido and the Dynamic Sphere by A. Westbrook and O. Ratti. (Rutland, Vt.: Tuttle, 1980.)

Are You a Target? by Judith Fein. (Belmont, Calif.: Wadsworth, 1981.)

Assault with a Deadly Weapon: The Autobiography of a Street Criminal by John Allen. D. H. Kelley and P. Heymann, eds. (New York: Pantheon, 1977.)

Avoiding Rape: A Study of Victims and Avoiders by Pauline Bart. National Institutes of Mental Health/U.S. Department of Health, Education, and Welfare. (Washington, D.C.: U.S. Government Printing Office, 1980.)

Body Language by Julius Fast. (New York: Simon & Schuster, 1970.)

The Complete Book of Locks, Keys, Burglar and Smoke Alarms, and Other Security Devices by Eugene A. Sloane. (New York: Morrow, 1977.)

Comprehensive Asian Fighting Arts by Donn F. Draeger and Robert W. Smith. (New York: Kodansha, 1980.)

Criminal Violence, Criminal Justice by Charles Silberman. (New York: Vintage, 1978.)

Defensible Space: Crime Prevention Through Urban Design by Oscar Newman. (New York: Collier, 1973.)

"The Figgie Report on Fear of Crime." (Ohio: A-T-O, Inc., 1980.)

The Function of the Police in Crisis Intervention and Conflict Management. Law Enforcement Assistance Administration/U.S. Department of Justice. (Washington D.C.: U.S. Government Printing Office, 1975.)

Giving In to Get Your Way by Terry Dobson and Victor Miller. (New York: Delacorte. 1978.)

The Gun in America by L. Kennett and J. Anderson. (Connecticut: Greenwood Press, 1975.)

Home Security. William Frankel, ed. (Alexandria, Va.: Time-Life Books, 1979.)

How to Avoid Burglary, Housebreaking, and Other Crimes by Ulrich Kaufmann. (New York: Crown, 1967.)

How to Protect Yourself from Crime by I. A. Lipman. (New York: Atheneum, 1975.)

In the Gravest Extreme: The Role of the Firearm in Civilian Defense by M. F. Ayoob.

Mugging: You Can Protect Yourself by Liddon R. Griffith. (Englewood, N.J.: Prentice-Hall, 1977.)

"On Being Mugged: The Event and Its Aftermath" by R. Lejeune and N. Alex in *Urban Life and Culture* (Vol. 2, No. 3), October 1973.

Personal and Family Safety and Crime Prevention by N. Olson. (New York: Holt, Rinehart & Winston, 1980.)

Principles of Personal Defense by Jeff Cooper. (Boulder, Colo.: Paladin Press, 1972.)

The Professional Fence by C. B. Klockars. (New York: Free Press, 1974.)

Rape: Prevention and Resistance. (San Francisco: Queen's Bench Foundation, 1976.)

Rape: The Crime and Its Prevention. Office of the Attorney General Crime Prevention Unit. California Department of Justice Information Pamphlet No. 12, 1978.

Research into Violent Behavior: Overview and Sexual Assaults. Subcommittee on Domestic and International Scientific Planning, Analysis, and Cooperation. (Washington, D.C.: U.S. Government Printing Office, 1978.)

Ripoffs by Robert Hendrickson. (New York: Viking, 1976.)

The Roots of Crime: What You Need to Know About Crime and What You Can Do About It by Eda Le Shan. (New York: Four Winds, 1981.)

Security! by Martin Clifford. (New York: Drake, 1974.)

Sexual Assualt: Confronting Rape in America by Nancy Gager and Cathleen Schurr. (New York: Grosset & Dunlap, 1976.)

The Silent Pulse by George Leonard. (New York: Dutton, 1978.)

The Stash Book by Peter Hjersman. (Berkeley, Calif.: And/Or Press, 1978.)

Survival in the City by Anthony Greenbank. (New York: Harper & Row, 1974.)

About the Authors

Terry Dobson is a nationally recognized expert in the areas of personal safety and conflict resolution. He provides security consultation for individuals and organizations and leads workshops and seminars in this area for major universities, corporations, and community groups. The author of *Giving In to Get Your Way,* he holds a fourth-degree black belt in Aikido, the Japanese nonviolent martial art. Mr. Dobson spent more than a decade in the Orient, where he apprenticed with the founder of the discipline.

Judith Shepherd-Chow teaches in the Social Work Education Department at San Francisco State University. She has supervised data collection in a national study on juvenile crime and has extensive experience in community development work and individual counseling. Ms. Shepherd-Chow holds a doctorate from the University of California at Berkeley.